the gospel of *john*

A **SIMPLY BIBLE** STUDY

CARMEN BEASLEY

I AM THE RESURRECTION
AND THE LIFE. WHOEVER
BELIEVES IN ME, THOUGH HE
DIE, YET SHALL HE LIVE...

JOHN 11:25

welcome!

SHARING GOD'S STORY OF **SIMPLY BIBLE**

Dear Friend,

WELCOME to *Simply Bible: The Gospel of John.* I'm thrilled you're here.

If it's okay, I'd like to share the culmination of ideas that led to this study. Warning: it's rather long-winded. My heart is to give you the big picture of the "why" for SIMPLY BIBLE.

It all began with a three-year plan. As a women's ministry director, my desire is:

> To inspire every woman to love God with all her heart, soul, mind, and strength, and to love others as herself. (Luke 10:27)

Basically, this means "love God with every part of our being and love others." But practically, what does that look like? Hence came a three-year plan to better understand our call:

YEAR ONE: Answer what does it mean to love and honor God and others with our bodies and our physical strength?

YEAR TWO: Zero in on heart issues. How do we love Him and others with our emotions and our wills? (Not that we women are especially emotional creatures!)

YEAR THREE: Dig into what it means to love and honor God and others with our minds. How do we take captive our "run away and run wild" thoughts?

To begin Year One with a focus on body issues, the gospel of John makes perfect sense.

WHY JOHN? John reveals the importance of the human body. Have you, like me, ever wondered why God put our souls in these flesh and blood bodies that get sick, age, fall apart, and turn to dust? Psalm 139 says we are "fearfully and wonderfully made," but I have yet to meet a woman who is completely thrilled with her own body.

Beyond that, why would God Himself take on a frail human body and then die? These concepts have serious implications for our own bodies, not to mention our entire being! Throughout his gospel, John emphasizes the humanity of Jesus, the Son of Man. From the beginning, he makes a big deal about Jesus taking on a body:

> And the Word became flesh and dwelt among us.
> *John 1:14*

Of course, John, an eyewitness to Jesus, has ever so much more to say about Him. Want to better know Him? Love Him? Trust Him? John has real answers. His Gospel applies directly to our everyday lives and is meant to be read and studied over and over again for that very purpose. At church and in our online community, we'll discuss these everyday body and soul issues related to John through Bible study and coffee chats. That's the reason for John.

WHY **SIMPLY BIBLE**? It's a fair question.

After much prayer and assessing women's ministries, God pointed to inductive study. (I'll share some things I learned about today's woman while assessing in just a bit.) Inductive study means directly studying the Bible. That's it. And so, the conversation looked like this:

Me: "Lord, You mean no video teaching and no fill-in-the-blank workbooks?"

God: "Yes. Take women directly to my Word."

Me: "Lord, women like to have a book in their hands, and preferably one from a well-known author."

God: "Use my Book."

So then, I obeyed. Ugh! I wish. Instead, I'm embarrassed to say that I played Gideon, setting my fleece out for God to prove His point. I purchased and reviewed every single Bible study available on the gospel of John. Almost desperately, I was looking for something - anything - that would quietly and inductively walk women through the Gospel of John. One by one, God said "no."

Okay, it's not like God audibly spoke to me. But His Spirit has a way of getting His message across. You know what I mean? I continued to cry out to Him for a tool. Frankly, for years, even as an experienced leader and Bible teacher, I've searched for a simple tool that does not require extra training in order to teach or study inductively. I could not find one.

One day, while wrestling with all of this, I sat down at my computer, opened a blank document and began experimenting with the process of inductive study. I left my computer and went down to fix dinner. When I returned, I looked at what was on the paper and thought, "This works." And I praised God!

I praise God for Melissa who has taken this material and made it something beautiful. The design is beyond anything I could have begun to think or imagine. I'm grateful.

FINALLY, WHY INDUCTIVE STUDY? There are three main reasons based on what today's woman says about Bible study:

FIRST: *"I feel inept. I know I should read the Bible. I really want to, but I just don't understand it."* Many women feel the same. With an influx of Bible study resources, we have relied on videos and study guides that give us the author's answers. It's easy to think we need an "expert" to intercede and interpret God's Word on our behalf. No doubt, there is a place for these resources, but we aren't to be dependent on them. We depend on God alone.

An old Chinese Proverb aptly says:

> Give a man a fish and you feed him for a day.
> Teach a man to fish and you feed him for a lifetime.

SIMPLY BIBLE is here to help and is designed to equip you to "fish." By following this step-by-step framework, you can confidently approach God's Word. The framework of this journal eliminates my voice as much as possible with the hopes that you can listen to God's voice.

That's the beauty of inductive study: rather than listening to an author, we listen directly to *the* Author. My prayer is that you will experience the incredible joy and adventure of personal encounters with Him through His Word and then share Him with others.

SECOND: *"I'm busy. Overwhelmed by demands. Life is crazy!"*
I know. I feel it too. This study should maximize time. Rather than spending time reading other books or watching videos, we skip the "middle-man" and go directly to God and His Word. Immediately, we relate with Him one-on-one rather than by filling in the blanks and checking Bible study off our "To Do" list.

Truly, this study can be catered to the needs of the busy mom who can barely scrape together ten minutes a day for Bible study. Yet, it can also fit the need of the woman who longs to linger and dig deep into the Word. Kind of like scuba diving, you'll choose how deep you want to go and how far you'd like to roam.

THIRD: *"I need relationship. Do others care about me?"*
Today's younger woman is seeking connection. Her desire? To be seen, known, and heard. Video teaching often does not meet her expressed need because it takes time from deeper relationship building - both with Christ and with others. Although she is hungry to know, the bottom line is she prefers personal interaction. And the discussion had better be relevant and meaningful, with no pat answers.

Concurrently, a generation of women my age are now dependent on video teachers and fill-in-the-blank studies, rather than dependent on God and His Word. Because of her dependency on these tools, a veteran Bible student is often ill-equipped to read the Bible for herself and even more ill-equipped to come alongside another in order to share her faith and God's Word.

Inductive study maximizes time and develops skills to focus on real relationship and interaction with God and others. Why SIMPLY BIBLE? To focus on the "relationship need" now felt acutely within women's ministries across the country.

CONSIDER FAST FOOD VERSUS A HOME-COOKED MEAL. Picking up fast food can be a treat. It's quick and easy. It's downright helpful to have someone else prepare and hand you the meal. Much of our Bible study resources are similar to "fast food." Someone else does the preparation and serves up a quick and easy word of encouragement. It's helpful, but it's not "home-cooked." Rarely would we serve fast food to friends or carry it to a potluck. The same holds true for feasting on God's Word. Inductive study allows for that special and intimate meal meant to be shared.

So that's a God-at-work story. That's the reason this series begins with John, the reason it uses inductive study, and the reason SIMPLY BIBLE was birthed. You've probably gathered by now that this study is different. And different often falls outside our comfort zones.

The purpose of this Bible study journal is that you may confidently read, understand, and apply God's Word like you've never before experienced, using simply the Bible. It will require a commitment.

My first home-cooked meal didn't taste or look anything like my mom's meal. Cooking takes practice. Even after forty-some years of cooking, most of what I cook tastes different from my mom's cooking. The same will be true for Bible study. Inductive study will take practice. Your study will look different from most others. You are unique and special. And so, your study insights and application will be unique.

JUST COMMIT. There's no "Oh, I'll just give it a try." Commit to a year of John. Commitments aren't easy. But by the end of this study, you will know Christ, His Word, and your identity in Him. You are loved, valued, and treasured by an amazing God. He came that you might believe.

I'm praying for you and with you.

With much love and joy,

Carmen

Lord God Almighty,

I PRAISE YOU FOR WHO YOU ARE. John tells us: "In the beginning was the Word, and the Word was with God, and the Word was God." You were in the beginning with God. All things were made through You, and without You was not anything made that was made. In You is life, and this life is the light of all mankind. Your light shines in the darkness, and the darkness has not overcome it.

You are the true light, which gives light to everyone in the world. All who receive You, who believe in Your name, are given the right to become children of God. Thank You! We praise You, Jesus! You are the Word made flesh, and You are full of grace and truth. From Your fullness we have all received, grace upon grace.

Lord God, we dedicate this study to You. As we open Your Word to the Gospel of John, please open our eyes, ears, minds, and hearts to better understand Your Word and to more fully know You. We surrender our all to You. Shine Your light in any dark crevice of our hearts and minds and souls, that we might walk in Your way.

Lead, guide, strengthen, and encourage each one of us as we learn new Bible study skills. I pray a hedge of protection over each sheep as she seeks to commit to know You through Your Word and this study. May nothing hinder her. Lord, reign victorious. Multiply the fruit of our study in ways that we could never think to ask or imagine. Unify our hearts with Yours and with one another.

Lord, we long to know and love You more and to better live out Your love. Ultimately, may our study bring glory and honor to Your Great Name. Jesus, all praise and glory to You.

ADD YOUR PERSPECTIVE TO OUR PRAYER. TELL GOD HOW YOU ARE FEELING AS YOU BEGIN THIS STUDY. ARE YOU EXCITED? AFRAID? GOD ALREADY KNOWS. BE REAL WITH HIM.

preparing the *net*

AN INTRODUCTION TO INDUCTIVE BIBLE STUDY

preparing the *net*

AN INTRODUCTION TO INDUCTIVE BIBLE STUDY

In order to fish, Christ's first disciples utilized a net. A big net! Similarly, the inductive study method will serve as our "net" to explore God's Word.

What is the inductive method? According to *The Westminster Dictionary of Theological Terms*, it's "the use of probable inferences as a means of coming to conclusions." Now before anyone jumps out of the boat, please keep in mind that we all utilize inductive reasoning every day. You and I already have the skills. We only need practice using them for Bible study.

The inductive Bible study method involves three parts that often overlap with one another (think net!): Observation, Interpretation, and Application.

1. OBSERVATION

Detectives always use inductive reasoning. For a while, my young adult children were somewhat obsessed with the current BBC version of *Sherlock* starring Benedict Cumberbatch. If you've ever watched it, you've *observed* Sherlock *observe* the facts. He looks carefully at all the details and asks questions concerning the who, what, when, where, why, and how.

Without thinking twice about it, we ourselves daily use observation skills, especially in relationships. We might notice that a co-worker is especially happy. We observe that she arrives on time, is smiling, has an extra kick to her step, cheerfully answers the phone, etc. Without coffee this is unusual morning behavior for her, and so, we are quick to note the time of day. More than likely, we will ask some questions to find out what's up. Inquiring minds want to know!

Moms are especially keen in observation skills. Beginning at birth, a mother will notice even the slightest change in the behavior of her baby. She knows if the little one is hungry, tired, or uncomfortable. How? Observation. Instinctively, she travels through a mental checklist and considers the time, the cry, the condition of the diaper, etc. No doubt! Moms seem to possess hidden powers of deduction that decipher the messages and needs of their children. Her "hidden powers" begin with observation. If you have a mom, you know this to be true.

We all use observation. By examining and asking questions, we can learn a lot about people and situations. This same idea applies to understanding God's Word. Observation means we read, study, and ask questions of the text. We want to know, "What does the Scripture say?"

2. INTERPRETATION

Careful observation leads to solid interpretation. Sherlock carefully observes the facts. This enables him to decipher or *interpret* the hidden clues. Similarly, moms who observe their babies learn to interpret the baby's messages. As we live daily life and go about our various relationships and activities, we often observe and interpret our observations simultaneously.

The same is true of the Bible. Observation and interpretation go hand-in-hand. As we carefully read and observe what the scripture says, we often understand and interpret it's meaning at the same time.

Other times, interpretation is not so easy. After all, the Bible was written in ancient times spanning the course of over two thousand years by people and to a people of utterly foreign cultures. Therefore, certain resources are handy. These tools help us properly interpret Scripture. (Think of a detective pulling out a fingerprint kit or a mom utilizing a thermometer. Tools help to more accurately assess a scenario.) For Bible study, tools can include:

- *Cross references:* Allowing Scripture to more accurately interpret scripture.
- *Word study:* Understanding the meaning of a word in its original language through the use of a concordance or Bible dictionary.
- *Other resources, including Bible dictionaries, handbooks and commentaries:* These help to verify our conclusions as well as provide historical or cultural context.

Careful observation and good interpretation help us answer: What does the Scripture say and what does it mean?

It's exciting when, together with the Holy Spirit's illumination, we are able to deduce the meaning of a passage. Oftentimes, finding these nuggets of truth, promises, and the revelation of God Himself literally takes my breath away! There is no other book like it:

> For the word of God is living and active, sharper than
> any two-edged sword, piercing to the division of soul and
> of spirit, of joints and of marrow, and discerning the
> thoughts and intentions of the heart.
> *Hebrews 4:12*

The God of the Universe loves us and personally reveals Himself through His Living Word. When He does, it cuts in a good way. Then we're ready to apply His Word to our everyday lives.

A SPECIAL NOTE: In discussing interpretation, it's important to remember that Scripture, in its original context, had one meaning. This makes sense in the context of Sherlock, right? There is only one right interpretation that will solve Sherlock's case. Similarly, this is true for mothers. Imagine a mom feeding her baby when in reality the diaper needed changing. Without careful observation and interpretation, the case is not solved!

With the Bible, the author had a specific message written at a specific time and a specific place for a specific group of people. Although we won't always be able to determine what the author's specific intent was, that is our goal. We want to know what did the author say and mean in that time and place in history? We try going back in time. If only there really was a "time machine!"

Not to be scary, but we humans are easily deceived. Without proper context, it's easy for us to take God's Word and make it say what we want it to say. The crafty serpent helped lead Eve to think wrongly about God's Word way back in the garden days:

> He [the serpent] said to the woman, "Did God actually
> say, 'You shall not eat of any tree in the garden'?"
> *Genesis 3:1*

The serpent goes on to help Eve interpret God's Word:

> But the serpent said to the woman, "You will not surely die.
> For God knows that when you eat of it your eyes will be
> opened, and you will be like God, knowing good and evil."
> *Genesis 3:4-5*

The result was, well, bad:

> So when the woman saw that the tree was good for food, and
> that it was a delight to the eyes, and that the tree was to be
> desired to make one wise, she took of its fruit and ate, and she
> also gave some to her husband who was with her, and he ate.
> *Genesis 3:6*

Lack of observation and wrong interpretation lead to bad application.

All that to say, the most important parts of inductive study are observation and interpretation, and these require the most time. When we do these well, the application step comes easily.

3. APPLICATION

Application is the fun and creative part. Although the original author of Scripture had one meaning, the personal applications of Scripture are many. This is personal. Between you and God. He may teach, correct, rebuke, or train. He is always equipping. (II Timothy 3:16-17) If we're willing, He will lead you to apply His Word specifically to your everyday life and needs.

I CAME THAT
THEY MAY HAVE LIFE
AND HAVE IT ABUNDANTLY.

JOHN 10:10

practice casting the *net*

OBSERVE, INTERPRET, APPLY

practice casting the *net*

OBSERVE, INTERPRET, APPLY

So far, all this inductive talk has been highly theoretical. Like riding a bike, you don't learn until you try. So let's do it!

Grab a Bible.

When I sit down with my Bible, I often think of it as a conversation with God, a prayer. He's speaking. I'm listening. He reveals Himself through His Word.

So pray. Pray before, during, and after reading. If practicing the presence of God is a new idea for you, you're in the right place. Simply tell God how you feel and ask Him to lead. Throughout your study time, continue leaning into Him.

Remember our big three? Observe, interpret, apply.

It's as simple as that. For practice, let's look at Mark's gospel account of Jesus. Open to Mark 1:1-8 and then…

OBSERVE

Read the passage carefully. This will be (and should be) the most time consuming part of the study. Ask questions of the text and highlight verses that touch your heart. If anything is especially noteworthy to you, jot it down on the practice worksheets provided in this journal. Keep in mind: this framework is simply a guide. You can fill in as little or as much of the space as you desire.

Here are some ideas to help you read carefully. Pick and choose or try them all:

- Read the passage.
- Read the passage in a different version.
- Read it out loud.
- Highlight or journal a verse that pops out to you.

- Go back and read it again while asking questions of the text. Nab the practice lesson sheets in the "Lesson Samples" section (beginning on page *xxxi*) and write down some of your questions and observations.
- Play detective and ask "who, what, when, where, how, or why."
- Note what took place before and after this passage.
- Notice repeated words and unfamiliar words. On your practice sheet, underline, circle, box, or highlight them. This is your place for notes.
- Watch for people and places.
- Mark places on a map.
- Listen to the passage while running errands.
- Ponder.
- Doodle or write out a verse in a journaling Bible.
- Ask God if there is anything else He'd like for you to notice.

INTERPRET

Okay. Great work! You've read and observed carefully. Now ask God to help you understand what the passage means.

One simple way to interpret is to answer the questions you've asked. Try answering them without the aid of study notes or other helps. If the answers are not intuitive or easily found within the scripture, there are tools available:

1. CROSS REFERENCES: Some Bibles offer cross references. This is a solid way to allow Scripture to interpret Scripture. Your Bible does not include cross references (most journaling Bibles do not)? No worries! It's very easy to access cross references online. Bible Hub is an easy place to access them. Here's a helpful link for Mark 1:1: **http://biblehub.com/mark/1-1.htm**. You'll see the cross reference section on the right-hand column of the page.

EXAMPLE: Mark 1:1 may have a small notation after "the Son of God" like this: ª. Notice that, either in the margin or at the bottom of the text, there will be a matching ª that notes a different Scripture reference. For Mark 1:1, the ESV shows: ª Matt. 14:33. Take a moment to look it up. By reading Matthew 14:33, we can confirm that the "Son of God" was another name referring to Jesus. Mark this on your practice sheet.

2. KEY WORDS: If you noticed a word that was repeated, define it. Perhaps you noticed an unfamiliar word or place. Look it up! God's Word leads us on an adventure.

EXAMPLE: *In Mark 1:1, the author uses the word "gospel." That's not a word that I use every day – how about you? If you grew up in church, you might be familiar with this term and can easily define or interpret it. Even so, I might look it up to be sure it means what I think it means. For definitions, we have options.*

- A simple way to define a word is to read the verse in another version. Rather than "gospel," the NIV reads "good news."

- My favorite way to define is to use a concordance. This book looks at words in their original language. I like the *Strong's Concordance*, which can also be found online. Going online? Try Blue Letter Bible: **https://www.blueletterbible.org/**

Once you're at Blue Letter Bible, simply type Mark 1:1 into the "Search the Bible" box. Click on the box called "TOOLS" next to Mark 1:1 and an assortment of choices will arrive. Find the corresponding Strong's Concordance number for "gospel" (in this case: G2098) and click on it. You'll retrieve the Greek word, original definitions, and how it is used in other places of the Bible. It's fascinating! Make note of your definitions on the practice sheet.

- In order to define people or places, Bible dictionaries are handy. Try: **www.biblegateway.com, www.blueletterbible.com,** or **www.biblehub.com**

3. OTHER RESOURCES: Finally, if you have time and want to dig, there are resources galore to help verify our conclusions: Bible dictionaries, handbooks, and commentaries. These enable us to better understand the cultural and historical context. Ideally, it's best to save these resources for last. Seek to understand God's Word on your own first.

Personally, I admire the dedication and genius of the scholars who write commentaries. These amazingly dedicated scholars study for the glory of God. However, they are not a substitute for reading God's Word on your own. First listen to God Himself.

Also, please note that commentaries are often written according to various theological bents. It's helpful to compare. Know your sources. This is especially crucial if roaming the Internet. Please surf with discernment.

APPLY (THE FINAL STEP!)

Ask God to help you apply His Word to your life. Oftentimes this happens while I observe and interpret. A particular verse or word or idea will strike a chord in my heart. If this happens, slow down. Take note. Ponder. Show God what you've discovered. This is the amazing process of God revealing Himself and His truths to you through His Word and the power of His Holy Spirit. Again, He may teach, correct, rebuke, or train. He is always equipping (II Timothy 3:16-17).

Enjoy being together with Him in His Word. Savor. Learn. Grow. Thank. Praise. Love.

Then carry a nugget of truth in your heart to ponder with Him as you go about your day.

YOU DID IT!

That's it. That's all there is to it. If this is your first time, the process surely felt tedious. Don't panic. You probably don't remember how clumsy and time consuming it was the very first time you tried tying your shoe or riding a bike or driving a car. Practice helps. Same for Bible study.

You're more observant, smarter, and stronger than you think you are. God created you that way. More importantly, He is with you. His desire is to be known. Lean into Him. Ask, seek, and you will find. His grace is sufficient. His power is made perfect in our weakness.

Friend, I'm so excited to be on this journey with you! I'm praying for you and will be cheering you onward. In fact, many women connected to our church's Women's Ministry are praying for you and will rally around you as we study together. Keep in mind that no one expects you to have all the answers. Weekly, we'll gather in small Bible study groups to read, compare notes, discuss and find answers to lingering questions. I encourage you to do the same. Bible study is best done within safe community where we can encourage one another in grace and truth. God uses "iron to sharpen iron." Be brave. Be strong. Together we will learn to love God and love one another.

Imagine His delight as we take baby steps in His direction. Imagine His joy and His "'Atta girl!"

Lord God, as we study Your Word, be our Good Shepherd. Open the eyes and ears of our hearts that we might we might follow Thee...

MY SHEEP HEAR MY VOICE,

AND I KNOW THEM,

AND THEY FOLLOW ME.

JOHN 10:27

examining *context*

BY THE SEA OF GALILEE

FOR FROM HIS FULLNESS
WE HAVE ALL RECEIVED,
GRACE UPON GRACE.

JOHN 1:16

examining *context*

BY THE SEA OF GALILEE

So much of Jesus's life and ministry took place around the Sea of Galilee. For primo Bible study, we've already discussed the importance of understanding the author's original intent or the meaning of the text to the ancient readers (or hearers) themselves. This section will help us keep important information found in the Gospel of John - people, places, and ideas - in context.

It includes a number of charts to store useful information that may be accessed quickly and easily. This begins with a place to draw a simple map of Israel (at least mine is simple!) Other helps, aids, or notes can be added as we go.

By the time we conclude our study, this section should provide a fairly good synopsis of John for easy review. The main point is to keep an overall perspective of the Gospel of John.

For now, here's what's included:

1. A *syllabus*.

2. Space to draw a *map of Israel* and mark all the **places mentioned in John.**

3. *Names of God* list: Record the various **names of God** used by John.

4. *'I AM'* statements: Mark the **"I am" statements used by Christ.**

5. A list of *'signs'*: Keep track of **Christ's miracles** here.

6. *'Truly, truly…'* Statements: Take note of these **important words of Jesus.**

7. *Themes* in the Gospel of John: List the various **themes used by John.** Like melodies in an orchestral piece, John refers to and repeats certain themes throughout his text. Here's a place to keep track of the Scripture references.

course *syllabus*

THE GOSPEL OF JOHN | LESSON SCHEDULE

WEEK	LESSON	SCRIPTURE
1	Introduction	Introduction
2	Lesson 1	John 1:1-18
3	Lesson 2	John 1:19-51
4	Lesson 3	John 2
5	Lesson 4	John 3
6	Lesson 5	John 4
7	Lesson 6	John 5
8	Lesson 7	John 6
9	Lesson 8	John 7:1-52
10	Lesson 9	John 7:53 - 8:59
11	Lesson 10	John 9
12	Lesson 11	John 10
13	Lesson 12	John 11
14	Lesson 13	John 12
15	Lesson 14	John 13
16	Lesson 15	John 14
17	Lesson 16	John 15
18	Lesson 17	John 16
19	Lesson 18	John 17
20	Lesson 19	John 18
21	Lesson 20	John 19
22	Lesson 21	John 20
23	Lesson 22	John 21
24	Lesson 23	Review

map of *Israel*

names of *God*

NAME	REFERENCE

"I Am" *statements*

I AM...		REFERENCE

list of *signs*

SIGN	REFERENCE

"truly" *statements*

TRULY, TRULY, I SAY...	REFERENCE

major themes in *john*

THEME	REFERENCES

major themes in *john*

THEME	REFERENCES

BEHOLD, THE LAMB OF
GOD, WHO TAKES AWAY
THE SIN OF THE WORLD!

JOHN 1:29

lesson *samples*

PRACTICE LESSONS & EXAMPLES

practice *lesson*

MARK 1:1-8 | TITLE: _____

READ	OBSERVE	INTERPRET
[1] The beginning of the gospel of Jesus Christ, the Son of God. [2] As it is written in Isaiah the prophet, "Behold, I send my messenger before your face, who will prepare your way, [3] the voice of one crying in the wilderness: 'Prepare the way of the Lord, make his paths straight,'" [4] John appeared, baptizing in the wilderness and proclaiming a baptism of repentance for the forgiveness of sins. [5] And all the country of Judea and all Jerusalem were going out to him and were being baptized by him in the river Jordan, confessing their sins. [6] Now John was clothed with camel's hair and wore a leather belt around his waist and ate locusts and wild honey. [7] And he preached, saying, "After me comes he who is mightier than I, the strap of whose sandals I am not worthy to stoop down and untie. [8] I have baptized you with water, but he will baptize you with the Holy Spirit."		

KEY WORDS	DEFINITIONS	CROSS REFERENCES

MAIN POINT(S)

APPLY

PRAY

sample *lesson*

MARK 1:1-8 | COMPLETED

READ	OBSERVE	INTERPRET

¹ The beginning of the gospel of Jesus Christ, the Son of God.
 	
² As it is written in Isaiah the prophet,
"Behold, I send my messenger before your face,
    who will prepare your way,
³ the voice of one crying in the wilderness:
    'Prepare the way of the Lord,
    make his paths straight,'"
 	
⁴ John appeared, baptizing in the wilderness and proclaiming a baptism of repentance for the forgiveness of sins. ⁵ And all the country of Judea and all Jerusalem were going out to him and were being baptized by him in the river Jordan, confessing their sins. ⁶ Now John was clothed with camel's hair and wore a leather belt around his waist and ate locusts and wild honey. ⁷ And he preached, saying, "After me comes he who is mightier than I, the strap of whose sandals I am not worthy to stoop down and untie. ⁸ I have baptized you with water, but he will baptize you with the Holy Spirit."
	What is the meaning of "gospel?"
	
	Find Jerusalem, Judea, and Jordan River on a map.
	
	Jesus, Isaiah, and John are the three main characters.
	
	What does it mean that John baptized with water?
		Gospel meant "good news," or more specifically, meant the good news of salvation through Jesus.
		
		Jesus: The Son of God
		Isaiah: a prophet
		John: the one Isaiah said would prepare the way of the Lord
		
		John's water baptism was a cleansing ceremony demonstrating repentance.

KEY WORDS	DEFINITIONS	CROSS REFERENCES
Gospel	Good news - NIV (https://www.biblegateway.com/resources/eastons-bible--dictionary/Gospel)	
Baptize	To cleanse by dipping or sub-merging, to make clean with water, to wash one's self, bathe. John's was a baptism of repentance & became ob-solete for Jesus's baptism that followed profession of faith in Him. (https://www.blueletterbible.org/lang/lexicon/lexicon.cfm?Strongs=G907&t=KJV)	**Acts 13:34** Before his coming, John had proclaimed a baptism of repen-tance to all the people of Israel. (http://biblehub.com/mark/1-1.htm)

MAIN POINT(S)

John the Baptist preaches repentance and baptizes people from Judea and Jerusalem who confess their sins. He says the one who is mighty and baptizes with the Holy Spirit is coming after Him.

APPLY

John the Baptist boldly proclaims the way of the Lord. Do I?

How can I better share the "good news" of Jesus?

John understood that Jesus was greater than himself. In what area of life do I need more

PRAY

Lord, I praise You for the Good News of Jesus, and for this account of John the Baptist. I see how boldly John confesses You to others. When I apply this to my life, I realize that I've not lived in this same way. I'm sorry for keeping Your good news to myself. Please help me to humbly share my faith with others. Amen.

a quick sample *lesson*

MARK 1:1-8 | FOR THOSE CRAZY, BUSY DAYS

READ	OBSERVE	INTERPRET
[1] The beginning of the gospel of Jesus Christ, the Son of God. [2] As it is written in Isaiah the prophet, "Behold, I send my messenger before your face, who will prepare your way, [3] the voice of one crying in the wilderness: 'Prepare the way of the Lord, make his paths straight,'" [4] John appeared, baptizing in the wilderness and proclaiming a baptism of repentance for the forgiveness of sins. [5] And all the country of Judea and all Jerusalem were going out to him and were being baptized by him in the river Jordan, confessing their sins. [6] Now John was clothed with camel's hair and wore a leather belt around his waist and ate locusts and wild honey. [7] And he preached, saying, "After me comes he who is mightier than I, the strap of whose sandals I am not worthy to stoop down and untie. [8] I have baptized you with water, but he will baptize you with the Holy Spirit."	What is the meaning of "gospel?"	Gospel meant "good news," or more specifically, meant the good news of salvation through Jesus.

KEY WORDS	DEFINITIONS	CROSS REFERENCES
Gospel	Good news *(https://www.biblegateway.com/resources/eastons-bible--dictionary/Gospel)*	

MAIN POINT(S)

The author of Mark begins his gospel or good news of Jesus telling about John the Baptist, who preaches and baptizes people from Judea and Jerusalem.

APPLY

I'd like to better understand the "good news" of Jesus.

PRAY

Lord God, I praise You for the Good News of Jesus. I thank You for Your Word. God, I really want to better understand Your Word and know You, Jesus. Please lead. And Lord, help me to remember that You and Your Good News go with me throughout this busy day. I want to walk hand in hand with You today.

a deeper sample *lesson*

MARK 1:1-8 | FOR THOSE DAYS WHEN YOU WANT TO DIG IN

READ

¹ The beginning of the gospel of Jesus Christ, the Son of God.

² As it is written in Isaiah the prophet,
"Behold, I send my messenger before your face,
who will prepare your way,
³ the voice of one crying in the wilderness:
'Prepare the way of the Lord, make his paths straight,'"

⁴ John appeared, baptizing in the wilderness and proclaiming a baptism of repentance for the forgiveness of sins. ⁵ And all the country of Judea and all Jerusalem were going out to him and were being baptized by him in the river Jordan, confessing their sins. ⁶ Now John was clothed with camel's hair and wore a leather belt around his waist and ate locusts and wild honey. ⁷ And he preached, saying, "After me comes he who is mightier than I, the strap of whose sandals I am not worthy to stoop down and untie. ⁸ I have baptized you with water, but he will baptize you with the Holy Spirit."

OBSERVE

When is the beginning of the gospel?

What is the meaning of "gospel?"

Who is Jesus? Why is He called the Son of God?

Who is Isaiah the prophet? When did he say this?

Behold, prepare, & make: imperative verbs

Who is John? Why is he baptizing in the wilderness?

Where is the wilderness?

What is a baptism of "repentance for the forgiveness of sins?"

Find Jerusalem, Judea, and Jordan River on a map.

What does it mean / look like to confess sins?

Why does John dress and eat this way?

Who is coming that is mightier than him?

What does it mean to baptize with water or with the Holy Spirit?

INTERPRET

Mark begins his account of Jesus with John the Baptist who is described centuries earlier by the prophet Isaiah (in the OT) as God's messenger who will prepare the way for the Lord. To the author, the gospel meant "good news," or more specifically, the good news of salvation through Jesus. Evidently, John's garments and food were common to desert dwellers at that time. John is preparing the way for Jesus by calling people to repent and be baptized, to admit their sin and turn back to the Lord. John's baptism was a cleansing ceremony demonstrating repentance. Christ's Holy Spirit baptism demonstrates the believer's faith in Jesus. A Christian baptism is a declaration to follow Christ as the way and the truth and the life.

xxxviii   the gospel of john • SIMPLY BIBLE

KEY WORDS	DEFINITIONS	CROSS REFERENCES
Gospel	Good news; the welcome intelligence of salvation to man as preached by our Lord and his followers.	**Rom. 1:16** For I am not ashamed of the gospel, for it is the power of God for salvation to everyone who believes, to the Jew first and also to the Greek.
Baptize	To cleanse by dipping or submerging, to make clean with water, to wash oneself, bathe. John's was a baptism of repentance & became obsolete for Jesus's baptism that followed a profession of faith in Him.	**Acts 13:34** Before his coming, John had proclaimed a baptism of repentance to all the people of Israel.

MAIN POINT(S)

Isaiah prophesies that John would come to "prepare the way of the Lord." John does appear, preaches for repentance and baptizes people from Judea and Jerusalem who confess their sins. He says the one who is mighty and baptizes with the Holy Spirit is coming after Him.

APPLY

John the Baptist boldly proclaims the way of the Lord. Do I?

John understood that Jesus was greater than himself. In what area do I need more humility?

Remember: I've been baptized by the Holy Spirit. Yield to Him!

PRAY

Lord, I thank You for how You have revealed Yourself throughout the ages. God, I see how boldly John confesses You to others. I realize that I've not lived this way. I'm sorry for keeping Your good news to myself. Please open a door for me to share it with someone this week. Thank You for the gift of Your Holy Spirit. May I live yielded to Him...

I AM THE RESURRECTION
AND THE LIFE. WHOEVER
BELIEVES IN ME, THOUGH HE
DIE, YET SHALL HE LIVE...

JOHN 11:25

week *one*

INTRODUCTION TO THE GOSPEL OF JOHN

take *note*

INTRODUCTION TO THE GOSPEL OF JOHN

take *note*

INTRODUCTION TO THE GOSPEL OF JOHN

take *note*

INTRODUCTION TO THE GOSPEL OF JOHN

take *note*

INTRODUCTION TO THE GOSPEL OF JOHN

take *note*

INTRODUCTION TO THE GOSPEL OF JOHN

take *note*

INTRODUCTION TO THE GOSPEL OF JOHN

take *note*

INTRODUCTION TO THE GOSPEL OF JOHN

take *note*

INTRODUCTION TO THE GOSPEL OF JOHN

take *note*

INTRODUCTION TO THE GOSPEL OF JOHN

take *note*

INTRODUCTION TO THE GOSPEL OF JOHN

IN THE BEGINNING WAS
THE WORD, AND THE
WORD WAS WITH GOD,
AND THE WORD WAS GOD..

JOHN 1:1

week *two*

---

day *one*

JOHN 1:1-5

READ	OBSERVE	INTERPRET
[1] In the beginning was the Word, and the Word was with God, and the Word was God. [2] He was in the beginning with God. [3] All things were made through him, and without him was not any thing made that was made. [4] In him was life, and the life was the light of men. [5] The light shines in the darkness, and the darkness has not overcome it.		

KEY WORDS	DEFINITIONS	CROSS REFERENCES

MAIN POINT(S)

APPLY

PRAY

day *two*

READ	OBSERVE	INTERPRET
6 There was a man sent from God, whose name was John. 7 He came as a witness, to bear witness about the light, that all might believe through him. 8 He was not the light, but came to bear witness about the light.		

KEY WORDS	DEFINITIONS	CROSS REFERENCES

MAIN POINT(S)	APPLY

PRAY

day *three*

JOHN 1:9-13

READ	OBSERVE	INTERPRET
⁹ The true light, which gives light to everyone, was coming into the world. ¹⁰ He was in the world, and the world was made through him, yet the world did not know him. ¹¹ He came to his own, and his own people did not receive him. ¹² But to all who did receive him, who believed in his name, he gave the right to become children of God, ¹³ who were born, not of blood nor of the will of the flesh nor of the will of man, but of God.		

KEY WORDS	DEFINITIONS	CROSS REFERENCES

MAIN POINT(S)

APPLY

PRAY

day *four*

JOHN 1:14-18

READ	OBSERVE	INTERPRET
¹⁴ And the Word became flesh and dwelt among us, and we have seen his glory, glory as of the only Son from the Father, full of grace and truth. ¹⁵ (John bore witness about him, and cried out, "This was he of whom I said, 'He who comes after me ranks before me, because he was before me.'") ¹⁶ For from his fullness we have all received, grace upon grace. ¹⁷ For the law was given through Moses; grace and truth came through Jesus Christ. ¹⁸ No one has ever seen God; the only God, who is at the Father's side, he has made him known.		

KEY WORDS	DEFINITIONS	CROSS REFERENCES

MAIN POINT(S)

APPLY

PRAY

day *five*

JOHN 1:1-18 | REVIEW & DISCUSSION QUESTIONS

Summary:	Write out a favorite verse(s) from the passage, perhaps in your own words:
Why do you think John begins his story of Jesus with a reference to creation: "in the beginning?"	How is *light* and *darkness* a reference to creation?
John refers to Jesus as The Word. Why is this significant?	Why do you think John stresses that the Word was and is God? (1:1-2, 1:18)

What is significant about "the Word became flesh?" (1:14)	Does this hold significance for our flesh and body?
What is the meaning of verse 12?	Can anyone become a child of God?
Have you personally received & believed in Christ? If so, what did that look like? If not or you are not sure, talk with God. Consider sharing your questions with a leader or trusted friend.	Praise God for at least one truth from this week's study:

THE LIGHT SHINES
IN THE DARKNESS,
AND THE DARKNESS
HAS NOT OVERCOME IT.

JOHN 1:5

week *three*

LESSON 2: JOHN 1:19-51

day *one*

JOHN 1:19-28

READ	OBSERVE	INTERPRET
¹⁹ And this is the testimony of John, when the Jews sent priests and Levites from Jerusalem to ask him, "Who are you?" ²⁰ He confessed, and did not deny, but confessed, "I am not the Christ." ²¹ And they asked him, "What then? Are you Elijah?" He said, "I am not." "Are you the Prophet?" And he answered, "No." ²² So they said to him, "Who are you? We need to give an answer to those who sent us. What do you say about yourself?" ²³ He said, "I am the voice of one crying out in the wilderness, 'Make straight the way of the Lord,' as the prophet Isaiah said." ²⁴ (Now they had been sent from the Pharisees.) ²⁵ They asked him, "Then why are you baptizing, if you are neither the Christ, nor Elijah, nor the Prophet?" ²⁶ John answered them, "I baptize with water, but among you stands one you do not know, ²⁷ even he who comes after me, the strap of whose sandal I am not worthy to untie." ²⁸ These things took place in Bethany across the Jordan, where John was baptizing.		

KEY WORDS	DEFINITIONS	CROSS REFERENCES

MAIN POINT(S)

APPLY

PRAY

day *two*

JOHN 1:29-34

READ	OBSERVE	INTERPRET
[29] The next day he saw Jesus coming toward him, and said, "Behold, the Lamb of God, who takes away the sin of the world! [30] This is he of whom I said, 'After me comes a man who ranks before me, because he was before me.' [31] I myself did not know him, but for this purpose I came baptizing with water, that he might be revealed to Israel." [32] And John bore witness: "I saw the Spirit descend from heaven like a dove, and it remained on him. [33] I myself did not know him, but he who sent me to baptize with water said to me, 'He on whom you see the Spirit descend and remain, this is he who baptizes with the Holy Spirit.' [34] And I have seen and have borne witness that this is the Son of God."		

KEY WORDS	DEFINITIONS	CROSS REFERENCES

MAIN POINT(S)

APPLY

PRAY

day *three*

JOHN 1:35-42

READ	OBSERVE	INTERPRET
³⁵ The next day again John was standing with two of his disciples, ³⁶ and he looked at Jesus as he walked by and said, "Behold, the Lamb of God!" ³⁷ The two disciples heard him say this, and they followed Jesus. ³⁸ Jesus turned and saw them following and said to them, "What are you seeking?" And they said to him, "Rabbi" (which means Teacher), "where are you staying?" ³⁹ He said to them, "Come and you will see." So they came and saw where he was staying, and they stayed with him that day, for it was about the tenth hour. ⁴⁰ One of the two who heard John speak and followed Jesus was Andrew, Simon Peter's brother. ⁴¹ He first found his own brother Simon and said to him, "We have found the Messiah" (which means Christ). ⁴² He brought him to Jesus. Jesus looked at him and said, "You are Simon the son of John. You shall be called Cephas" (which means Peter).		

KEY WORDS	DEFINITIONS	CROSS REFERENCES

MAIN POINT(S)

APPLY

PRAY

day *four*

JOHN 1:43-51

READ	OBSERVE	INTERPRET
[43] The next day Jesus decided to go to Galilee. He found Philip and said to him, "Follow me." [44] Now Philip was from Bethsaida, the city of Andrew and Peter. [45] Philip found Nathanael and said to him, "We have found him of whom Moses in the Law and also the prophets wrote, Jesus of Nazareth, the son of Joseph." [46] Nathanael said to him, "Can anything good come out of Nazareth?" Philip said to him, "Come and see." [47] Jesus saw Nathanael coming toward him and said of him, "Behold, an Israelite indeed, in whom there is no deceit!" [48] Nathanael said to him, "How do you know me?" Jesus answered him, "Before Philip called you, when you were under the fig tree, I saw you." [49] Nathanael answered him, "Rabbi, you are the Son of God! You are the King of Israel!" [50] Jesus answered him, "Because I said to you, 'I saw you under the fig tree,' do you believe? You will see greater things than these." [51] And he said to him, "Truly, truly, I say to you, you will see heaven opened, and the angels of God ascending and descending on the Son of Man."		

KEY WORDS	DEFINITIONS	CROSS REFERENCES

MAIN POINT(S)

APPLY

PRAY

day *five*

JOHN 1:19-51 | REVIEW & DISCUSSION QUESTIONS

Summary:	Write out a favorite verse(s) from the passage, perhaps in your own words:
How does John the Baptist respond to the religious leaders?	What does this tell you about him?
What most intrigues you about John the Baptist? What's the purpose of his baptizing people with water? (1:31)	John the Baptist calls Jesus the "Lamb of God." (1:29) How does that name fit?

Jesus points to Genesis 28:12 in verse 51. Why?	Why does Jesus call Himself "Son of Man?"
How would you define the role of a disciple? Are you following Jesus as a disciple?	Specifically, what does being a disciple look like in your life? How does that compare to the disciples in John 1:19-51?
Is there anyone in your life that you might invite to "come and see" Jesus? How could you extend an invitation?	Praise God for at least one truth from this week's study:

"COME AND SEE…"

JOHN 1:46

week *four*

LESSON 3: JOHN 2

day *one*

JOHN 2:1-11

READ	OBSERVE	INTERPRET
¹ On the third day there was a wedding at Cana in Galilee, and the mother of Jesus was there. ² Jesus also was invited to the wedding with his disciples. ³ When the wine ran out, the mother of Jesus said to him, "They have no wine." ⁴ And Jesus said to her, "Woman, what does this have to do with me? My hour has not yet come." ⁵ His mother said to the servants, "Do whatever he tells you." ⁶ Now there were six stone water jars there for the Jewish rites of purification, each holding twenty or thirty gallons. ⁷ Jesus said to the servants, "Fill the jars with water." And they filled them up to the brim. ⁸ And he said to them, "Now draw some out and take it to the master of the feast." So they took it. ⁹ When the master of the feast tasted the water now become wine, and did not know where it came from (though the servants who had drawn the water knew), the master of the feast called the bridegroom ¹⁰ and said to him, "Everyone serves the good wine first, and when people have drunk freely, then the poor wine. But you have kept the good wine until now." ¹¹ This, the first of his signs, Jesus did at Cana in Galilee, and manifested his glory. And his disciples believed in him.		

KEY WORDS	DEFINITIONS	CROSS REFERENCES

MAIN POINT(S)

APPLY

PRAY

day *two*

READ	OBSERVE	INTERPRET
[12] After this he went down to Capernaum, with his mother and his brothers and his disciples, and they stayed there for a few days. [13] The Passover of the Jews was at hand, and Jesus went up to Jerusalem. [14] In the temple he found those who were selling oxen and sheep and pigeons, and the money-changers sitting there. [15] And making a whip of cords, he drove them all out of the temple, with the sheep and oxen. And he poured out the coins of the money-changers and overturned their tables. [16] And he told those who sold the pigeons, "Take these things away; do not make my Father's house a house of trade." [17] His disciples remembered that it was written, "Zeal for your house will consume me."		

KEY WORDS	DEFINITIONS	CROSS REFERENCES

MAIN POINT(S)

APPLY

PRAY

day *three*

JOHN 2:18-22

READ	OBSERVE	INTERPRET
[18] So the Jews said to him, "What sign do you show us for doing these things?" [19] Jesus answered them, "Destroy this temple, and in three days I will raise it up." [20] The Jews then said, "It has taken forty-six years to build this temple, and will you raise it up in three days?" [21] But he was speaking about the temple of his body. [22] When therefore he was raised from the dead, his disciples remembered that he had said this, and they believed the Scripture and the word that Jesus had spoken.		

KEY WORDS	DEFINITIONS	CROSS REFERENCES

MAIN POINT(S)

APPLY

PRAY

day *four*

JOHN 2:23-25

READ	OBSERVE	INTERPRET
23 Now when he was in Jerusalem at the Passover Feast, many believed in his name when they saw the signs that he was doing. 24 But Jesus on his part did not entrust himself to them, because he knew all people 25 and needed no one to bear witness about man, for he himself knew what was in man.		

KEY WORDS	DEFINITIONS	CROSS REFERENCES

MAIN POINT(S)

APPLY

PRAY

day *five*

JOHN 2 | REVIEW & DISCUSSION QUESTIONS

Summary:	Write out a favorite verse(s) from the passage, perhaps in your own words:
What stands out to you about the first sign Jesus performs?	What does this miracle tell you about Christ's transforming power?
Similarly, how does the image of a wedding tell us what's in store for God's people?	How did this first sign affect the disciples?

From the scene in the temple, what do you learn about Jesus?	Jesus calls the temple "My Father's House." What does He reveal about Himself?
How do you think others would have reacted to this scene in the temple?	Why does John add verses 21 and 22 to his record of Jesus? Why would this reference to Christ's physical body be important to John?
What insight is most meaningful to you in this chapter?	Praise God for at least one truth from this week's study:

JESUS ANSWERED THEM,
"DESTROY THIS TEMPLE,
AND IN THREE DAYS
I WILL RAISE IT UP."

JOHN 2:19

week *five*

LESSON 4: JOHN 3

day *one*

JOHN 3:1-8

READ	OBSERVE	INTERPRET
[1] Now there was a man of the Pharisees named Nicodemus, a ruler of the Jews. [2] This man came to Jesus by night and said to him, "Rabbi, we know that you are a teacher come from God, for no one can do these signs that you do unless God is with him." [3] Jesus answered him, "Truly, truly, I say to you, unless one is born again he cannot see the kingdom of God." [4] Nicodemus said to him, "How can a man be born when he is old? Can he enter a second time into his mother's womb and be born?" [5] Jesus answered, "Truly, truly, I say to you, unless one is born of water and the Spirit, he cannot enter the kingdom of God. [6] That which is born of the flesh is flesh, and that which is born of the Spirit is spirit. [7] Do not marvel that I said to you, 'You must be born again.' [8] The wind blows where it wishes, and you hear its sound, but you do not know where it comes from or where it goes. So it is with everyone who is born of the Spirit.		

KEY WORDS	DEFINITIONS	CROSS REFERENCES

MAIN POINT(S)

APPLY

PRAY

day *two*

JOHN 3:9-15

READ	OBSERVE	INTERPRET
⁹ Nicodemus said to him, "How can these things be?" ¹⁰ Jesus answered him, "Are you the teacher of Israel and yet you do not understand these things? ¹¹ Truly, truly, I say to you, we speak of what we know, and bear witness to what we have seen, but you do not receive our testimony. ¹² If I have told you earthly things and you do not believe, how can you believe if I tell you heavenly things? ¹³ No one has ascended into heaven except he who descended from heaven, the Son of Man. ¹⁴ And as Moses lifted up the serpent in the wilderness, so must the Son of Man be lifted up, ¹⁵ that whoever believes in him may have eternal life.		

KEY WORDS	DEFINITIONS	CROSS REFERENCES

MAIN POINT(S)

APPLY

PRAY

day *three*

JOHN 3:16-21

READ	OBSERVE	INTERPRET
[16] "For God so loved the world, that he gave his only Son, that whoever believes in him should not perish but have eternal life. [17] For God did not send his Son into the world to condemn the world, but in order that the world might be saved through him. [18] Whoever believes in him is not condemned, but whoever does not believe is condemned already, because he has not believed in the name of the only Son of God. [19] And this is the judgment: the light has come into the world, and people loved the darkness rather than the light because their works were evil. [20] For everyone who does wicked things hates the light and does not come to the light, lest his works should be exposed. [21] But whoever does what is true comes to the light, so that it may be clearly seen that his works have been carried out in God."		

KEY WORDS	DEFINITIONS	CROSS REFERENCES

MAIN POINT(S)

APPLY

PRAY

day *four*

READ

²² After this Jesus and his disciples went into the Judean countryside, and he remained there with them and was baptizing. ²³ John also was baptizing at Aenon near Salim, because water was plentiful there, and people were coming and being baptized ²⁴ (for John had not yet been put in prison).

²⁵ Now a discussion arose between some of John's disciples and a Jew over purification. ²⁶ And they came to John and said to him, "Rabbi, he who was with you across the Jordan, to whom you bore witness—look, he is baptizing, and all are going to him." ²⁷ John answered, "A person cannot receive even one thing unless it is given him from heaven. ²⁸ You yourselves bear me witness, that I said, 'I am not the Christ, but I have been sent before him.' ²⁹ The one who has the bride is the bridegroom. The friend of the bridegroom, who stands and hears him, rejoices greatly at the bridegroom's voice. Therefore, this joy of mine is now complete. ³⁰ He must increase, but I must decrease." ³¹ He who comes from above is above all. He who is of the earth belongs to the earth and speaks in an earthly way. He who comes from heaven is above all. ³² He bears witness to what he has seen and heard, yet no one receives his testimony. ³³ Whoever receives his testimony sets his seal to this, that God is true. ³⁴ For he whom God has sent utters the words of God, for he gives the Spirit without measure. ³⁵ The Father loves the Son and has given all things into his hand. ³⁶ Whoever believes in the Son has eternal life; whoever does not obey the Son shall not see life, but the wrath of God remains on him.

OBSERVE

INTERPRET

KEY WORDS	DEFINITIONS	CROSS REFERENCES

MAIN POINT(S)

APPLY

PRAY

day *five*

JOHN 3 | REVIEW & DISCUSSION QUESTIONS

Summary:	Write out a favorite verse(s) from the passage, perhaps in your own words:
Who is Nicodemus? What do you think his purpose is in coming to Jesus?	In verse 3, Jesus tells Nicodemus, "You must be born again." In your own words, how do you explain the meaning of "you must be born again?"
Jesus refers to Moses lifting up a serpent in verse 14. This reference comes from Numbers 21:4-9. What is the connection?	Jesus already knows His mission (3:14-15). What is His mission and why is it necessary?

In Christ's conversation with Nicodemus, what insights did you glean concerning the role of the Spirit?

What do we learn about God the Father in John 3:16-17? Please share your personal thoughts about God's actions.

True or False: Based on Jesus' teaching, living a good, moral life will lead to eternal life. Support your answer with Scripture.

What words and attitudes of John the Baptist impress you? Specifically, how can you seek to apply his example to your own life?

John again discusses light and darkness in this chapter. Personally, are there areas in your own life that you would prefer God not shine His light? Why? Honestly talk to God about these things.

Praise God for at least one truth from this week's study:

TRULY, TRULY, I SAY TO YOU, UNLESS ONE IS BORN OF WATER AND THE SPIRIT, HE CANNOT ENTER THE KINGDOM OF GOD.

JOHN 3:5

week six

LESSON 5: JOHN 4

day *one*

JOHN 4:1-15

READ

¹ Now when Jesus learned that the Pharisees had heard that Jesus was making and baptizing more disciples than John ² (although Jesus himself did not baptize, but only his disciples), ³ he left Judea and departed again for Galilee. ⁴ And he had to pass through Samaria. ⁵ So he came to a town of Samaria called Sychar, near the field that Jacob had given to his son Joseph. ⁶ Jacob's well was there; so Jesus, wearied as he was from his journey, was sitting beside the well. It was about the sixth hour.

⁷ A woman from Samaria came to draw water. Jesus said to her, "Give me a drink." ⁸ (For his disciples had gone away into the city to buy food.) ⁹ The Samaritan woman said to him, "How is it that you, a Jew, ask for a drink from me, a woman of Samaria?" (For Jews have no dealings with Samaritans.) ¹⁰ Jesus answered her, "If you knew the gift of God, and who it is that is saying to you, 'Give me a drink,' you would have asked him, and he would have given you living water." ¹¹ The woman said to him, "Sir, you have nothing to draw water with, and the well is deep. Where do you get that living water? ¹² Are you greater than our father Jacob? He gave us the well and drank from it himself, as did his sons and his livestock." ¹³ Jesus said to her, "Everyone who drinks of this water will be thirsty again, ¹⁴ but whoever drinks of the water that I will give him will never be thirsty again. The water that I will give him will become in him a spring of water welling up to eternal life." ¹⁵ The woman said to him, "Sir, give me this water, so that I will not be thirsty or have to come here to draw water."

OBSERVE

INTERPRET

KEY WORDS	DEFINITIONS	CROSS REFERENCES

MAIN POINT(S)

APPLY

PRAY

day *two*

JOHN 4:16-30

READ

16 Jesus said to her, "Go, call your husband, and come here." 17 The woman answered him, "I have no husband." Jesus said to her, "You are right in saying, 'I have no husband'; 18 for you have had five husbands, and the one you now have is not your husband. What you have said is true." 19 The woman said to him, "Sir, I perceive that you are a prophet. 20 Our fathers worshiped on this mountain, but you say that in Jerusalem is the place where people ought to worship." 21 Jesus said to her, "Woman, believe me, the hour is coming when neither on this mountain nor in Jerusalem will you worship the Father. 22 You worship what you do not know; we worship what we know, for salvation is from the Jews. 23 But the hour is coming, and is now here, when the true worshipers will worship the Father in spirit and truth, for the Father is seeking such people to worship him. 24 God is spirit, and those who worship him must worship in spirit and truth." 25 The woman said to him, "I know that Messiah is coming (he who is called Christ). When he comes, he will tell us all things." 26 Jesus said to her, "I who speak to you am he." 27 Just then his disciples came back. They marveled that he was talking with a woman, but no one said, "What do you seek?" or, "Why are you talking with her?" 28 So the woman left her water jar and went away into town and said to the people, 29 "Come, see a man who told me all that I ever did. Can this be the Christ?" 30 They went out of the town and were coming to him.

OBSERVE

INTERPRET

KEY WORDS	DEFINITIONS	CROSS REFERENCES

MAIN POINT(S)

APPLY

PRAY

day *three*

JOHN 4:31-45

READ

[31] Meanwhile the disciples were urging him, saying, "Rabbi, eat." [32] But he said to them, "I have food to eat that you do not know about." [33] So the disciples said to one another, "Has anyone brought him something to eat?" [34] Jesus said to them, "My food is to do the will of him who sent me and to accomplish his work. [35] Do you not say, 'There are yet four months, then comes the harvest'? Look, I tell you, lift up your eyes, and see that the fields are white for harvest. [36] Already the one who reaps is receiving wages and gathering fruit for eternal life, so that sower and reaper may rejoice together. [37] For here the saying holds true, 'One sows and another reaps.' [38] I sent you to reap that for which you did not labor. Others have labored, and you have entered into their labor."

[39] Many Samaritans from that town believed in him because of the woman's testimony, "He told me all that I ever did." [40] So when the Samaritans came to him, they asked him to stay with them, and he stayed there two days. [41] And many more believed because of his word. [42] They said to the woman, "It is no longer because of what you said that we believe, for we have heard for ourselves, and we know that this is indeed the Savior of the world."

[43] After the two days he departed for Galilee. [44] (For Jesus himself had testified that a prophet has no honor in his own hometown.) [45] So when he came to Galilee, the Galileans welcomed him, having seen all that he had done in Jerusalem at the feast. For they too had gone to the feast.

OBSERVE

INTERPRET

KEY WORDS	DEFINITIONS	CROSS REFERENCES

MAIN POINT(S)

APPLY

PRAY

day *four*

READ	OBSERVE	INTERPRET
[46] So he came again to Cana in Galilee, where he had made the water wine. And at Capernaum there was an official whose son was ill. [47] When this man heard that Jesus had come from Judea to Galilee, he went to him and asked him to come down and heal his son, for he was at the point of death. [48] So Jesus said to him, "Unless you see signs and wonders you will not believe." [49] The official said to him, "Sir, come down before my child dies." [50] Jesus said to him, "Go; your son will live." The man believed the word that Jesus spoke to him and went on his way. [51] As he was going down, his servants met him and told him that his son was recovering. [52] So he asked them the hour when he began to get better, and they said to him, "Yesterday at the seventh hour the fever left him." [53] The father knew that was the hour when Jesus had said to him, "Your son will live." And he himself believed, and all his household. [54] This was now the second sign that Jesus did when he had come from Judea to Galilee.		

KEY WORDS	DEFINITIONS	CROSS REFERENCES

MAIN POINT(S)

APPLY

PRAY

day *five*

JOHN 4 | REVIEW & DISCUSSION QUESTIONS

Summary:	Write out a favorite verse(s) from the passage, perhaps in your own words:
How does Jesus behave toward Samaritans? Toward women?	In your world, who are the Samaritans? What do you learn from Jesus that you might apply?
How would you describe the "living water?"	Why do some Jews miss out on the "living water?"

Why does Jesus mention that God is Spirit?	What does it mean to worship in "spirit and truth?"
What name do the Samaritans use to describe Jesus? (4:42) Why is this significant?	What impresses you concerning the Samaritan woman? What lessons can you apply to your own life?
Jesus seems to challenge the father seeking healing on behalf of his son? What do you think Christ desires for this man?	Praise God for at least one truth from this week's study:

...WHOEVER DRINKS OF THE
WATER THAT I WILL GIVE
HIM WILL NEVER BE THIRSTY
AGAIN. THE WATER THAT I
WILL GIVE HIM WILL BECOME
IN HIM A SPRING OF WATER
WELLING UP TO ETERNAL LIFE..

JOHN 4:14

week *seven*

LESSON 6: JOHN 5

day *one*

JOHN 5:1-9

READ	OBSERVE	INTERPRET
[1] After this there was a feast of the Jews, and Jesus went up to Jerusalem. [2] Now there is in Jerusalem by the Sheep Gate a pool, in Aramaic called Bethesda, which has five roofed colonnades. [3] In these lay a multitude of invalids—blind, lame, and paralyzed. [5] One man was there who had been an invalid for thirty-eight years. [6] When Jesus saw him lying there and knew that he had already been there a long time, he said to him, "Do you want to be healed?" [7] The sick man answered him, "Sir, I have no one to put me into the pool when the water is stirred up, and while I am going another steps down before me." [8] Jesus said to him, "Get up, take up your bed, and walk." [9] And at once the man was healed, and he took up his bed and walked.		

KEY WORDS	DEFINITIONS	CROSS REFERENCES

MAIN POINT(S)

APPLY

PRAY

day *two*

JOHN 5:10-18

READ	OBSERVE	INTERPRET
Now that day was the Sabbath. [10] So the Jews said to the man who had been healed, "It is the Sabbath, and it is not lawful for you to take up your bed." [11] But he answered them, "The man who healed me, that man said to me, 'Take up your bed, and walk.'" [12] They asked him, "Who is the man who said to you, 'Take up your bed and walk'?" [13] Now the man who had been healed did not know who it was, for Jesus had withdrawn, as there was a crowd in the place. [14] Afterward Jesus found him in the temple and said to him, "See, you are well! Sin no more, that nothing worse may happen to you." [15] The man went away and told the Jews that it was Jesus who had healed him. [16] And this was why the Jews were persecuting Jesus, because he was doing these things on the Sabbath. [17] But Jesus answered them, "My Father is working until now, and I am working." [18] This was why the Jews were seeking all the more to kill him, because not only was he breaking the Sabbath, but he was even calling God his own Father, making himself equal with God.		

KEY WORDS	DEFINITIONS	CROSS REFERENCES

MAIN POINT(S)

APPLY

PRAY

day *three*

JOHN 5:19-29

READ

¹⁹ So Jesus said to them, "Truly, truly, I say to you, the Son can do nothing of his own accord, but only what he sees the Father doing. For whatever the Father does, that the Son does likewise. ²⁰ For the Father loves the Son and shows him all that he himself is doing. And greater works than these will he show him, so that you may marvel. ²¹ For as the Father raises the dead and gives them life, so also the Son gives life to whom he will. ²² For the Father judges no one, but has given all judgment to the Son, ²³ that all may honor the Son, just as they honor the Father. Whoever does not honor the Son does not honor the Father who sent him. ²⁴ Truly, truly, I say to you, whoever hears my word and believes him who sent me has eternal life. He does not come into judgment, but has passed from death to life.

²⁵ "Truly, truly, I say to you, an hour is coming, and is now here, when the dead will hear the voice of the Son of God, and those who hear will live. ²⁶ For as the Father has life in himself, so he has granted the Son also to have life in himself. ²⁷ And he has given him authority to execute judgment, because he is the Son of Man. ²⁸ Do not marvel at this, for an hour is coming when all who are in the tombs will hear his voice ²⁹ and come out, those who have done good to the resurrection of life, and those who have done evil to the resurrection of judgment.

OBSERVE

INTERPRET

KEY WORDS	DEFINITIONS	CROSS REFERENCES

MAIN POINT(S)	APPLY

PRAY

day *four*

READ

³⁰ "I can do nothing on my own. As I hear, I judge, and my judgment is just, because I seek not my own will but the will of him who sent me. ³¹ If I alone bear witness about myself, my testimony is not true. ³² There is another who bears witness about me, and I know that the testimony that he bears about me is true. ³³ You sent to John, and he has borne witness to the truth. ³⁴ Not that the testimony that I receive is from man, but I say these things so that you may be saved. ³⁵ He was a burning and shining lamp, and you were willing to rejoice for a while in his light. ³⁶ But the testimony that I have is greater than that of John. For the works that the Father has given me to accomplish, the very works that I am doing, bear witness about me that the Father has sent me. ³⁷ And the Father who sent me has himself borne witness about me. His voice you have never heard, his form you have never seen, ³⁸ and you do not have his word abiding in you, for you do not believe the one whom he has sent. ³⁹ You search the Scriptures because you think that in them you have eternal life; and it is they that bear witness about me, ⁴⁰ yet you refuse to come to me that you may have life. ⁴¹ I do not receive glory from people. ⁴² But I know that you do not have the love of God within you. ⁴³ I have come in my Father's name, and you do not receive me. If another comes in his own name, you will receive him. ⁴⁴ How can you believe, when you receive glory from one another and do not seek the glory that comes from the only God? ⁴⁵ Do not think that I will accuse you to the Father. There is one who accuses you: Moses, on whom you have set your hope. ⁴⁶ For if you believed Moses, you would believe me; for he wrote of me. ⁴⁷ But if you do not believe his writings, how will you believe my words?"

OBSERVE

INTERPRET

KEY WORDS	DEFINITIONS	CROSS REFERENCES

MAIN POINT(S)

APPLY

PRAY

day *five*

JOHN 5 | REVIEW & DISCUSSION QUESTIONS

Summary:	Write out a favorite verse(s) from the passage, perhaps in your own words:
Why would Jesus ask the invalid, "Do you want to get well?" Are there reasons a sick person may not want to be fully well?	How might this same thinking apply to your own life? Does a particular area or stubborn sin come to mind? Seek God now.
How did Jesus cure the sick man?	Why are the Jews upset by this amazing miracle?

Consider the reaction of the Jews. Are there any areas where you also struggle with legalistic views? What would be an appropriate response?	In 5:31-47, Jesus lists a number of "witnesses" that "testify" to His identity. List them here:
What do you learn about Jesus "the Son" in this chapter?	What do you learn about God, "The Father" in this chapter?
Ponder verse 39. What are your thoughts? Consider again the reaction of the Jews.	Praise God for at least one truth from this week's study:

FOR AS THE FATHER HAS
LIFE IN HIMSELF, SO HE
HAS GRANTED THE SON ALSO
TO HAVE LIFE IN HIMSELF.

JOHN 5:26

week *eight*

LESSON 7: JOHN 6

day *one*

JOHN 6:1-14

READ

¹ After this Jesus went away to the other side of the Sea of Galilee, which is the Sea of Tiberias. ² And a large crowd was following him, because they saw the signs that he was doing on the sick. ³ Jesus went up on the mountain, and there he sat down with his disciples. ⁴ Now the Passover, the feast of the Jews, was at hand. ⁵ Lifting up his eyes, then, and seeing that a large crowd was coming toward him, Jesus said to Philip, "Where are we to buy bread, so that these people may eat?" ⁶ He said this to test him, for he himself knew what he would do. ⁷ Philip answered him, "Two hundred denarii worth of bread would not be enough for each of them to get a little." ⁸ One of his disciples, Andrew, Simon Peter's brother, said to him, ⁹ "There is a boy here who has five barley loaves and two fish, but what are they for so many?" ¹⁰ Jesus said, "Have the people sit down." Now there was much grass in the place. So the men sat down, about five thousand in number. ¹¹ Jesus then took the loaves, and when he had given thanks, he distributed them to those who were seated. So also the fish, as much as they wanted. ¹² And when they had eaten their fill, he told his disciples, "Gather up the leftover fragments, that nothing may be lost." ¹³ So they gathered them up and filled twelve baskets with fragments from the five barley loaves left by those who had eaten. ¹⁴ When the people saw the sign that he had done, they said, "This is indeed the Prophet who is to come into the world!"

OBSERVE

INTERPRET

KEY WORDS	DEFINITIONS	CROSS REFERENCES

MAIN POINT(S)

APPLY

PRAY

day *two*

JOHN 6:15-21

READ	OBSERVE	INTERPRET
¹⁵ Perceiving then that they were about to come and take him by force to make him king, Jesus withdrew again to the mountain by himself. ¹⁶ When evening came, his disciples went down to the sea, ¹⁷ got into a boat, and started across the sea to Capernaum. It was now dark, and Jesus had not yet come to them. ¹⁸ The sea became rough because a strong wind was blowing. ¹⁹ When they had rowed about three or four miles, they saw Jesus walking on the sea and coming near the boat, and they were frightened. ²⁰ But he said to them, "It is I; do not be afraid." ²¹ Then they were glad to take him into the boat, and immediately the boat was at the land to which they were going.		

KEY WORDS	DEFINITIONS	CROSS REFERENCES

MAIN POINT(S)

APPLY

PRAY

FOR THIS IS THE WILL OF
MY FATHER, THAT EVERYONE
WHO LOOKS ON THE SON
AND BELIEVES IN HIM SHOULD
HAVE ETERNAL LIFE...

JOHN 6:40

day *three*

READ

²² On the next day the crowd that remained on the other side of the sea saw that there had been only one boat there, and that Jesus had not entered the boat with his disciples, but that his disciples had gone away alone. ²³ Other boats from Tiberias came near the place where they had eaten the bread after the Lord had given thanks. ²⁴ So when the crowd saw that Jesus was not there, nor his disciples, they themselves got into the boats and went to Capernaum, seeking Jesus.

²⁵ When they found him on the other side of the sea, they said to him, "Rabbi, when did you come here?" ²⁶ Jesus answered them, "Truly, truly, I say to you, you are seeking me, not because you saw signs, but because you ate your fill of the loaves. ²⁷ Do not work for the food that perishes, but for the food that endures to eternal life, which the Son of Man will give to you. For on him God the Father has set his seal." ²⁸ Then they said to him, "What must we do, to be doing the works of God?" ²⁹ Jesus answered them, "This is the work of God, that you believe in him whom he has sent." ³⁰ So they said to him, "Then what sign do you do, that we may see and believe you? What work do you perform? ³¹ Our fathers ate the manna in the wilderness; as it is written, 'He gave them bread from heaven to eat.'" ³² Jesus then said to them, "Truly, truly, I say to you, it was not Moses who gave you the bread from heaven, but my Father gives you the true bread from heaven. ³³ For the bread of God is he who comes down from heaven and gives life to the world." ³⁴ They said to him, "Sir, give us this bread always."

³⁵ Jesus said to them, "I am the bread of life; whoever comes to me shall not hunger, and whoever believes in me shall never thirst. ³⁶ But I said to you that you have seen me and yet do not believe. ³⁷ All that the Father gives me will come to me, and whoever comes to me I will never cast out. ³⁸ For I have come down from heaven, not to do my own will but the will of him who sent me. ³⁹ And this is the will of him who sent me, that I should lose nothing of all that he has given me, but raise it up on the last day. ⁴⁰ For this is the will of my Father, that everyone who looks on the Son and believes in him should have eternal life, and I will raise him up on the last day."

⁴¹ So the Jews grumbled about him, because he said, "I am the bread that came down from heaven." ⁴² They said, "Is not this Jesus, the son of Joseph, whose father and mother we know? How does he now say, 'I have come down from heaven'?" ⁴³ Jesus answered them, "Do not grumble among yourselves. ⁴⁴ No one can come to me unless the Father who sent me draws him. And I will raise him up on the last day. ⁴⁵ It is written in the Prophets, 'And they will all be taught by God.' Everyone who has heard and learned from the Father comes to me— ⁴⁶ not that anyone has seen the Father except

SIMPLY BIBLE • the gospel of john   91

READ	OBSERVE	INTERPRET
he who is from God; he has seen the Father. ⁴⁷ Truly, truly, I say to you, whoever believes has eternal life. ⁴⁸ I am the bread of life. ⁴⁹ Your fathers ate the manna in the wilderness, and they died. ⁵⁰ This is the bread that comes down from heaven, so that one may eat of it and not die. ⁵¹ I am the living bread that came down from heaven. If anyone eats of this bread, he will live forever. And the bread that I will give for the life of the world is my flesh."		

KEY WORDS	DEFINITIONS	CROSS REFERENCES

MAIN POINT(S)

APPLY

PRAY

day *four*

READ	OBSERVE
⁵²The Jews then disputed among themselves, saying, "How can this man give us his flesh to eat?" ⁵³So Jesus said to them, "Truly, truly, I say to you, unless you eat the flesh of the Son of Man and drink his blood, you have no life in you. ⁵⁴Whoever feeds on my flesh and drinks my blood has eternal life, and I will raise him up on the last day. ⁵⁵For my flesh is true food, and my blood is true drink. ⁵⁶Whoever feeds on my flesh and drinks my blood abides in me, and I in him. ⁵⁷As the living Father sent me, and I live because of the Father, so whoever feeds on me, he also will live because of me. ⁵⁸This is the bread that came down from heaven, not like the bread the fathers ate, and died. Whoever feeds on this bread will live forever." ⁵⁹Jesus said these things in the synagogue, as he taught at Capernaum.	

⁶⁰When many of his disciples heard it, they said, "This is a hard saying; who can listen to it?" ⁶¹But Jesus, knowing in himself that his disciples were grumbling about this, said to them, "Do you take offense at this? ⁶²Then what if you were to see the Son of Man ascending to where he was before? ⁶³It is the Spirit who gives life; the flesh is no help at all. The words that I have spoken to you are spirit and life. ⁶⁴But there are some of you who do not believe." (For Jesus knew from the beginning who those were who did not believe, and who it was who would betray him.) ⁶⁵And he said, "This is why I told you that no one can come to me unless it is granted him by the Father."

INTERPRET

⁶⁶After this many of his disciples turned back and no longer walked with him. ⁶⁷So Jesus said to the twelve, "Do you want to go away as well?" ⁶⁸Simon Peter answered him, "Lord, to whom shall we go? You have the words of eternal life, ⁶⁹and we have believed, and have come to know, that you are the Holy One of God." ⁷⁰Jesus answered them, "Did I not choose you, the twelve? And yet one of you is a devil." ⁷¹He spoke of Judas the son of Simon Iscariot, for he, one of the twelve, was going to betray him.

KEY WORDS	DEFINITIONS	CROSS REFERENCES

MAIN POINT(S)

APPLY

PRAY

day *five*

Summary:	Write out a favorite verse(s) from the passage, perhaps in your own words:
What intrigues you concerning Jesus's question in verse 5?	How might Philip, Andrew, and the other disciples have felt?
What lessons do you take away from Jesus feeding the 5000?	Why do you think the crowds followed Jesus across the sea? How are we similar?

Jesus clearly speaks the Father's will for the people (6:29). What is it? Explain whether or not this is easy and why.	The Jews "grumble" about Jesus, and some of His disciples turn away. Why?
Why do the Twelve remain with Jesus?	List events, words, or names from John 6 that connect back to Exodus in some way.
John 6 is packed full of God's truth. What lesson do you most want to hold onto and apply to your own life?	Praise God for at least one truth from this week's study:

I AM THE BREAD OF LIFE.

JOHN 6:48

week *nine*

LESSON 8: JOHN 7:1-52

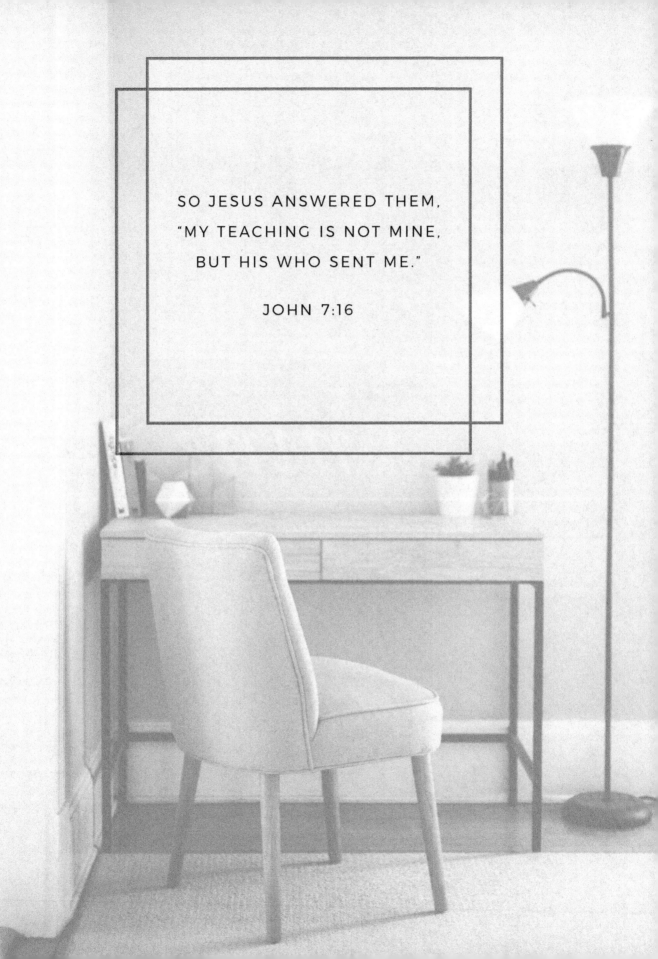

SO JESUS ANSWERED THEM,
"MY TEACHING IS NOT MINE,
BUT HIS WHO SENT ME."

JOHN 7:16

day *one*

READ

¹ After this Jesus went about in Galilee. He would not go about in Judea, because the Jews were seeking to kill him. ² Now the Jews' Feast of Booths was at hand. ³ So his brothers said to him, "Leave here and go to Judea, that your disciples also may see the works you are doing. ⁴ For no one works in secret if he seeks to be known openly. If you do these things, show yourself to the world." ⁵ For not even his brothers believed in him. ⁶ Jesus said to them, "My time has not yet come, but your time is always here. ⁷ The world cannot hate you, but it hates me because I testify about it that its works are evil. ⁸ You go up to the feast. I am not going up to this feast, for my time has not yet fully come." ⁹ After saying this, he remained in Galilee.

¹⁰ But after his brothers had gone up to the feast, then he also went up, not publicly but in private. ¹¹ The Jews were looking for him at the feast, and saying, "Where is he?" ¹² And there was much muttering about him among the people. While some said, "He is a good man," others said, "No, he is leading the people astray." ¹³ Yet for fear of the Jews no one spoke openly of him.

¹⁴ About the middle of the feast Jesus went up into the temple and began teaching. ¹⁵ The Jews therefore marveled, saying, "How is it that this man has learning, when he has never studied?" ¹⁶ So Jesus answered them, "My teaching is not mine, but his who sent me. ¹⁷ If anyone's will is to do God's will, he will know whether the teaching is from God or whether I am speaking on my own authority. ¹⁸ The one who speaks on his own authority seeks his own glory; but the one who seeks the glory of him who sent him is true, and in him there is no falsehood. ¹⁹ Has not Moses given you the law? Yet none of you keeps the law. Why do you seek to kill me?" ²⁰ The crowd answered, "You have a demon! Who is seeking to kill you?" ²¹ Jesus answered them, "I did one work, and you all marvel at it. ²² Moses gave you circumcision (not that it is from Moses, but from the fathers), and you circumcise a man on the Sabbath. ²³ If on the Sabbath a man receives circumcision, so that the law of Moses may not be broken, are you angry with me because on the Sabbath I made a man's whole body well? ²⁴ Do not judge by appearances, but judge with right judgment."

OBSERVE

INTERPRET

KEY WORDS	DEFINITIONS	CROSS REFERENCES

MAIN POINT(S)

APPLY

PRAY

day *two*

JOHN 7:25-31

READ	OBSERVE	INTERPRET
[25] Some of the people of Jerusalem therefore said, "Is not this the man whom they seek to kill? [26] And here he is, speaking openly, and they say nothing to him! Can it be that the authorities really know that this is the Christ? [27] But we know where this man comes from, and when the Christ appears, no one will know where he comes from." [28] So Jesus proclaimed, as he taught in the temple, "You know me, and you know where I come from. But I have not come of my own accord. He who sent me is true, and him you do not know. [29] I know him, for I come from him, and he sent me." [30] So they were seeking to arrest him, but no one laid a hand on him, because his hour had not yet come. [31] Yet many of the people believed in him. They said, "When the Christ appears, will he do more signs than this man has done?"		

KEY WORDS	DEFINITIONS	CROSS REFERENCES

MAIN POINT(S)

APPLY

PRAY

day *three*

JOHN 7:32-39

READ	OBSERVE	INTERPRET
³² The Pharisees heard the crowd muttering these things about him, and the chief priests and Pharisees sent officers to arrest him. ³³ Jesus then said, "I will be with you a little longer, and then I am going to him who sent me. ³⁴ You will seek me and you will not find me. Where I am you cannot come." ³⁵ The Jews said to one another, "Where does this man intend to go that we will not find him? Does he intend to go to the Dispersion among the Greeks and teach the Greeks? ³⁶ What does he mean by saying, 'You will seek me and you will not find me,' and, 'Where I am you cannot come'?" ³⁷ On the last day of the feast, the great day, Jesus stood up and cried out, "If anyone thirsts, let him come to me and drink. ³⁸ Whoever believes in me, as the Scripture has said, 'Out of his heart will flow rivers of living water.'" ³⁹ Now this he said about the Spirit, whom those who believed in him were to receive, for as yet the Spirit had not been given, because Jesus was not yet glorified.		

KEY WORDS	DEFINITIONS	CROSS REFERENCES

MAIN POINT(S)

APPLY

PRAY

day *four*

JOHN 7:40-52

READ	OBSERVE	INTERPRET
⁴⁰ When they heard these words, some of the people said, "This really is the Prophet." ⁴¹ Others said, "This is the Christ." But some said, "Is the Christ to come from Galilee? ⁴² Has not the Scripture said that the Christ comes from the offspring of David, and comes from Bethlehem, the village where David was?" ⁴³ So there was a division among the people over him. ⁴⁴ Some of them wanted to arrest him, but no one laid hands on him. ⁴⁵ The officers then came to the chief priests and Pharisees, who said to them, "Why did you not bring him?" ⁴⁶ The officers answered, "No one ever spoke like this man!" ⁴⁷ The Pharisees answered them, "Have you also been deceived? ⁴⁸ Have any of the authorities or the Pharisees believed in him? ⁴⁹ But this crowd that does not know the law is accursed." ⁵⁰ Nicodemus, who had gone to him before, and who was one of them, said to them, ⁵¹ "Does our law judge a man without first giving him a hearing and learning what he does?" ⁵² They replied, "Are you from Galilee too? Search and see that no prophet arises from Galilee."		

KEY WORDS	DEFINITIONS	CROSS REFERENCES

MAIN POINT(S)	APPLY

PRAY

day *five*

Summary:	Write out a favorite verse(s) from the passage, perhaps in your own words:
Contrast the differing attitudes of Jesus and His brothers.	Jesus appears to be the "talk of the town" at the festival. What's the dispute?
Jesus does go to the temple to teach. The Jews are impressed by His teaching. How does Jesus say His teaching can be tested? (7:17) Does this have implications to the hearers?	What is needed to proclaim Jesus today? (7:18) How might this challenge you?

How does Jesus back up His right to heal on the Sabbath? (7:21-24) What do you make of this?	The Jews seem to judge Jesus based on "appearances." What is the dispute? How should they determine His identity? How does this apply to you today?
Explain verses 37-39.	The officers return to the Pharisees without Jesus. What is their reason? What do you imagine they heard?
What do you make of Nicodemus in this chapter? What is ironic about his statement in verse 51?	Praise God for at least one truth from this week's study:

IF ANYONE THIRSTS, LET
HIM COME TO ME AND DRINK.

JOHN 7:37

week *ten*

LESSON 9: JOHN 7:53 - 8:59

day *one*

READ	OBSERVE	INTERPRET
⁵³ They went each to his own house, ¹ but Jesus went to the Mount of Olives. ² Early in the morning he came again to the temple. All the people came to him, and he sat down and taught them. ³ The scribes and the Pharisees brought a woman who had been caught in adultery, and placing her in the midst ⁴ they said to him, "Teacher, this woman has been caught in the act of adultery. ⁵ Now in the Law, Moses commanded us to stone such women. So what do you say?" ⁶ This they said to test him, that they might have some charge to bring against him. Jesus bent down and wrote with his finger on the ground. ⁷ And as they continued to ask him, he stood up and said to them, "Let him who is without sin among you be the first to throw a stone at her." ⁸ And once more he bent down and wrote on the ground. ⁹ But when they heard it, they went away one by one, beginning with the older ones, and Jesus was left alone with the woman standing before him. ¹⁰ Jesus stood up and said to her, "Woman, where are they? Has no one condemned you?" ¹¹ She said, "No one, Lord." And Jesus said, "Neither do I condemn you; go, and from now on sin no more."		

KEY WORDS	DEFINITIONS	CROSS REFERENCES

MAIN POINT(S)

APPLY

PRAY

day *two*

JOHN 8:12-30

READ	OBSERVE
¹² Again Jesus spoke to them, saying, "I am the light of the world. Whoever follows me will not walk in darkness, but will have the light of life." ¹³ So the Pharisees said to him, "You are bearing witness about yourself; your testimony is not true." ¹⁴ Jesus answered, "Even if I do bear witness about myself, my testimony is true, for I know where I came from and where I am going, but you do not know where I come from or where I am going. ¹⁵ You judge according to the flesh; I judge no one. ¹⁶ Yet even if I do judge, my judgment is true, for it is not I alone who judge, but I and the Father who sent me. ¹⁷ In your Law it is written that the testimony of two people is true. ¹⁸ I am the one who bears witness about myself, and the Father who sent me bears witness about me." ¹⁹ They said to him therefore, "Where is your Father?" Jesus answered, "You know neither me nor my Father. If you knew me, you would know my Father also." ²⁰ These words he spoke in the treasury, as he taught in the temple; but no one arrested him, because his hour had not yet come.	

	INTERPRET
²¹ So he said to them again, "I am going away, and you will seek me, and you will die in your sin. Where I am going, you cannot come." ²² So the Jews said, "Will he kill himself, since he says, 'Where I am going, you cannot come'?" ²³ He said to them, "You are from below; I am from above. You are of this world; I am not of this world. ²⁴ I told you that you would die in your sins, for unless you believe that I am he you will die in your sins." ²⁵ So they said to him, "Who are you?" Jesus said to them, "Just what I have been telling you from the beginning. ²⁶ I have much to say about you and much to judge, but he who sent me is true, and I declare to the world what I have heard from him." ²⁷ They did not understand that he had been speaking to them about the Father. ²⁸ So Jesus said to them, "When you have lifted up the Son of Man, then you will know that I am he, and that I do nothing on my own authority, but speak just as the Father taught me. ²⁹ And he who sent me is with me. He has not left me alone, for I always do the things that are pleasing to him." ³⁰ As he was saying these things, many believed in him.	

KEY WORDS	DEFINITIONS	CROSS REFERENCES

MAIN POINT(S)	APPLY

PRAY

day *three*

JOHN 8:31-47

READ

³¹ So Jesus said to the Jews who had believed him, "If you abide in my word, you are truly my disciples, ³² and you will know the truth, and the truth will set you free." ³³ They answered him, "We are offspring of Abraham and have never been enslaved to anyone. How is it that you say, 'You will become free'?"

³⁴ Jesus answered them, "Truly, truly, I say to you, everyone who practices sin is a slave to sin. ³⁵ The slave does not remain in the house forever; the son remains forever. ³⁶ So if the Son sets you free, you will be free indeed. ³⁷ I know that you are offspring of Abraham; yet you seek to kill me because my word finds no place in you. ³⁸ I speak of what I have seen with my Father, and you do what you have heard from your father."

³⁹ They answered him, "Abraham is our father." Jesus said to them, "If you were Abraham's children, you would be doing the works Abraham did, ⁴⁰ but now you seek to kill me, a man who has told you the truth that I heard from God. This is not what Abraham did. ⁴¹ You are doing the works your father did." They said to him, "We were not born of sexual immorality. We have one Father—even God." ⁴² Jesus said to them, "If God were your Father, you would love me, for I came from God and I am here. I came not of my own accord, but he sent me. ⁴³ Why do you not understand what I say? It is because you cannot bear to hear my word. ⁴⁴ You are of your father the devil, and your will is to do your father's desires. He was a murderer from the beginning, and does not stand in the truth, because there is no truth in him. When he lies, he speaks out of his own character, for he is a liar and the father of lies. ⁴⁵ But because I tell the truth, you do not believe me. ⁴⁶ Which one of you convicts me of sin? If I tell the truth, why do you not believe me? ⁴⁷ Whoever is of God hears the words of God. The reason why you do not hear them is that you are not of God."

OBSERVE

INTERPRET

KEY WORDS	DEFINITIONS	CROSS REFERENCES

MAIN POINT(S)

APPLY

PRAY

day *four*

READ

⁴⁸ The Jews answered him, "Are we not right in saying that you are a Samaritan and have a demon?" ⁴⁹ Jesus answered, "I do not have a demon, but I honor my Father, and you dishonor me. ⁵⁰ Yet I do not seek my own glory; there is One who seeks it, and he is the judge. ⁵¹ Truly, truly, I say to you, if anyone keeps my word, he will never see death." ⁵² The Jews said to him, "Now we know that you have a demon! Abraham died, as did the prophets, yet you say, 'If anyone keeps my word, he will never taste death.' ⁵³ Are you greater than our father Abraham, who died? And the prophets died! Who do you make yourself out to be?" ⁵⁴ Jesus answered, "If I glorify myself, my glory is nothing. It is my Father who glorifies me, of whom you say, 'He is our God.' ⁵⁵ But you have not known him. I know him. If I were to say that I do not know him, I would be a liar like you, but I do know him and I keep his word. ⁵⁶ Your father Abraham rejoiced that he would see my day. He saw it and was glad." ⁵⁷ So the Jews said to him, "You are not yet fifty years old, and have you seen Abraham?" ⁵⁸ Jesus said to them, "Truly, truly, I say to you, before Abraham was, I am." ⁵⁹ So they picked up stones to throw at him, but Jesus hid himself and went out of the temple.

OBSERVE

INTERPRET

KEY WORDS	DEFINITIONS	CROSS REFERENCES

MAIN POINT(S)

APPLY

PRAY

day *five*

Summary:	Write out a favorite verse(s) from the passage, perhaps in your own words:
Share your reaction and insights concerning Jesus, the Pharisees, and the woman caught in adultery?	Rather than condemn, Jesus exhorts the woman caught in adultery: "Go and from now on sin no more." Whether giving or receiving, what do you learn about forgiveness?
From Jesus's teaching, what does it mean to "walk in darkness?"	What does Jesus mean that He is "the light of the world?" Does this give hope or frighten you? Why?

What makes a true disciple? (8:31)	Ponder verse 36. Are there any areas of your life still needing the freedom of Christ? Based on Christ's teaching, what is necessary for freedom from any sin?
How does Jesus describe Satan? How have you seen this role of Satan play out in your own life?	What phrase does Jesus repeat in verses 24, 28, and 58? Why are the Jews upset by this? Share your own thoughts.
Jesus shares several promises in this chapter. Which one means the most to you today? (8:12, 32, 51)	Praise God for at least one truth from this week's study:

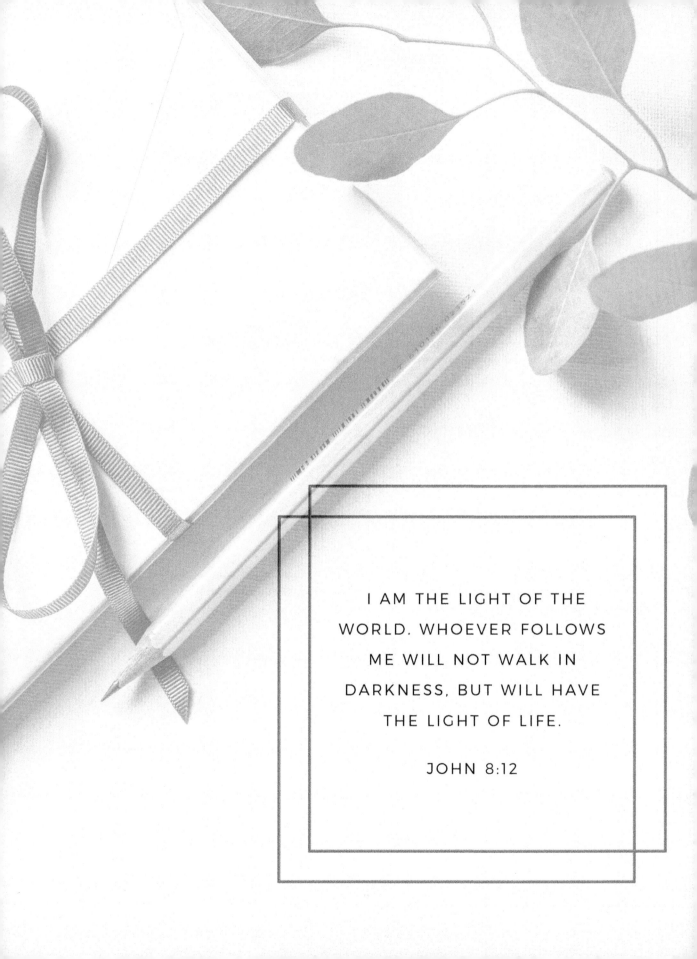

I AM THE LIGHT OF THE WORLD. WHOEVER FOLLOWS ME WILL NOT WALK IN DARKNESS, BUT WILL HAVE THE LIGHT OF LIFE.

JOHN 8:12

week *eleven*

LESSON 10: JOHN 9

day *one*

JOHN 9:1-7

READ	OBSERVE	INTERPRET
[1] As he passed by, he saw a man blind from birth. [2] And his disciples asked him, "Rabbi, who sinned, this man or his parents, that he was born blind?" [3] Jesus answered, "It was not that this man sinned, or his parents, but that the works of God might be displayed in him. [4] We must work the works of him who sent me while it is day; night is coming, when no one can work. [5] As long as I am in the world, I am the light of the world." [6] Having said these things, he spit on the ground and made mud with the saliva. Then he anointed the man's eyes with the mud [7] and said to him, "Go, wash in the pool of Siloam" (which means Sent). So he went and washed and came back seeing.		

KEY WORDS	DEFINITIONS	CROSS REFERENCES

MAIN POINT(S)

APPLY

PRAY

day *two*

JOHN 9:8-17

READ	OBSERVE	INTERPRET
[8] The neighbors and those who had seen him before as a beggar were saying, "Is this not the man who used to sit and beg?" [9] Some said, "It is he." Others said, "No, but he is like him." He kept saying, "I am the man." [10] So they said to him, "Then how were your eyes opened?" [11] He answered, "The man called Jesus made mud and anointed my eyes and said to me, 'Go to Siloam and wash.' So I went and washed and received my sight." [12] They said to him, "Where is he?" He said, "I do not know."		
[13] They brought to the Pharisees the man who had formerly been blind. [14] Now it was a Sabbath day when Jesus made the mud and opened his eyes. [15] So the Pharisees again asked him how he had received his sight. And he said to them, "He put mud on my eyes, and I washed, and I see."		
[16] Some of the Pharisees said, "This man is not from God, for he does not keep the Sabbath." But others said, "How can a man who is a sinner do such signs?" And there was a division among them. [17] So they said again to the blind man, "What do you say about him, since he has opened your eyes?" He said, "He is a prophet."		

KEY WORDS	DEFINITIONS	CROSS REFERENCES

MAIN POINT(S)

APPLY

PRAY

day *three*

JOHN 9:18-34

READ

¹⁸ The Jews did not believe that he had been blind and had received his sight, until they called the parents of the man who had received his sight ¹⁹ and asked them, "Is this your son, who you say was born blind? How then does he now see?" ²⁰ His parents answered, "We know that this is our son and that he was born blind. ²¹ But how he now sees we do not know, nor do we know who opened his eyes. Ask him; he is of age. He will speak for himself." ²² (His parents said these things because they feared the Jews, for the Jews had already agreed that if anyone should confess Jesus to be Christ, he was to be put out of the synagogue.) ²³ Therefore his parents said, "He is of age; ask him."

²⁴ So for the second time they called the man who had been blind and said to him, "Give glory to God. We know that this man is a sinner." ²⁵ He answered, "Whether he is a sinner I do not know. One thing I do know, that though I was blind, now I see." ²⁶ They said to him, "What did he do to you? How did he open your eyes?" ²⁷ He answered them, "I have told you already, and you would not listen. Why do you want to hear it again? Do you also want to become his disciples?" ²⁸ And they reviled him, saying, "You are his disciple, but we are disciples of Moses. ²⁹ We know that God has spoken to Moses, but as for this man, we do not know where he comes from." ³⁰ The man answered, "Why, this is an amazing thing! You do not know where he comes from, and yet he opened my eyes. ³¹ We know that God does not listen to sinners, but if anyone is a worshiper of God and does his will, God listens to him. ³² Never since the world began has it been heard that anyone opened the eyes of a man born blind. ³³ If this man were not from God, he could do nothing." ³⁴ They answered him, "You were born in utter sin, and would you teach us?" And they cast him out.

OBSERVE

INTERPRET

KEY WORDS	DEFINITIONS	CROSS REFERENCES

MAIN POINT(S)

APPLY

PRAY

day *four*

JOHN 9:35-41

READ	OBSERVE	INTERPRET
³⁵ Jesus heard that they had cast him out, and having found him he said, "Do you believe in the Son of Man?" ³⁶ He answered, "And who is he, sir, that I may believe in him?" ³⁷ Jesus said to him, "You have seen him, and it is he who is speaking to you." ³⁸ He said, "Lord, I believe," and he worshiped him. ³⁹ Jesus said, "For judgment I came into this world, that those who do not see may see, and those who see may become blind." ⁴⁰ Some of the Pharisees near him heard these things, and said to him, "Are we also blind?" ⁴¹ Jesus said to them, "If you were blind, you would have no guilt; but now that you say, 'We see,' your guilt remains.		

KEY WORDS	DEFINITIONS	CROSS REFERENCES

MAIN POINT(S)

APPLY

PRAY

day *five*

JOHN 9 | REVIEW & DISCUSSION QUESTIONS

Summary:	Write out a favorite verse(s) from the passage, perhaps in your own words:
Concerning disabilities, the disciple's question in verse 2 reveals what thoughts?	How does Jesus correct their thinking?
How does Jesus's view of disabilities challenge your own thinking?	How can God use your own brokenness to display His glory?

What testimony does the blind man give concerning Jesus?	What testimony do the blind man's parents give? Why?
What can we learn from the blind man and his parents about giving testimony to Jesus's work in our own lives?	The blind man's view of Jesus expands. Record how he refers to Jesus in verses 11, 17, 33, and 38. What do you notice? Thoughts?
How are the Pharisees blind? What lessons are we to take away from their blindness?	Praise God for at least one truth from this week's study:

JESUS ANSWERED, "IT WAS
NOT THAT THIS MAN SINNED,
OR HIS PARENTS, BUT THAT
THE WORKS OF GOD MIGHT BE
DISPLAYED IN HIM.

JOHN 9:3

week *twelve*

LESSON 11: JOHN 10

day *one*

JOHN 10:1-10

READ	OBSERVE	INTERPRET
[1] "Truly, truly, I say to you, he who does not enter the sheepfold by the door but climbs in by another way, that man is a thief and a robber. [2] But he who enters by the door is the shepherd of the sheep. [3] To him the gatekeeper opens. The sheep hear his voice, and he calls his own sheep by name and leads them out. [4] When he has brought out all his own, he goes before them, and the sheep follow him, for they know his voice. [5] A stranger they will not follow, but they will flee from him, for they do not know the voice of strangers." [6] This figure of speech Jesus used with them, but they did not understand what he was saying to them. [7] So Jesus again said to them, "Truly, truly, I say to you, I am the door of the sheep. [8] All who came before me are thieves and robbers, but the sheep did not listen to them. [9] I am the door. If anyone enters by me, he will be saved and will go in and out and find pasture. [10] The thief comes only to steal and kill and destroy. I came that they may have life and have it abundantly.		

KEY WORDS	DEFINITIONS	CROSS REFERENCES

MAIN POINT(S)

APPLY

PRAY

day *two*

JOHN 10:11-21

READ	OBSERVE	INTERPRET
¹¹ I am the good shepherd. The good shepherd lays down his life for the sheep. ¹² He who is a hired hand and not a shepherd, who does not own the sheep, sees the wolf coming and leaves the sheep and flees, and the wolf snatches them and scatters them. ¹³ He flees because he is a hired hand and cares nothing for the sheep. ¹⁴ I am the good shepherd. I know my own and my own know me, ¹⁵ just as the Father knows me and I know the Father; and I lay down my life for the sheep. ¹⁶ And I have other sheep that are not of this fold. I must bring them also, and they will listen to my voice. So there will be one flock, one shepherd. ¹⁷ For this reason the Father loves me, because I lay down my life that I may take it up again. ¹⁸ No one takes it from me, but I lay it down of my own accord. I have authority to lay it down, and I have authority to take it up again. This charge I have received from my Father." ¹⁹ There was again a division among the Jews because of these words. ²⁰ Many of them said, "He has a demon, and is insane; why listen to him?" ²¹ Others said, "These are not the words of one who is oppressed by a demon. Can a demon open the eyes of the blind?"		

KEY WORDS	DEFINITIONS	CROSS REFERENCES

MAIN POINT(S)

APPLY

PRAY

day *three*

JOHN 10:22-30

READ	OBSERVE	INTERPRET
²² At that time the Feast of Dedication took place at Jerusalem. It was winter, ²³ and Jesus was walking in the temple, in the colonnade of Solomon. ²⁴ So the Jews gathered around him and said to him, "How long will you keep us in suspense? If you are the Christ, tell us plainly." ²⁵ Jesus answered them, "I told you, and you do not believe. The works that I do in my Father's name bear witness about me, ²⁶ but you do not believe because you are not among my sheep. ²⁷ My sheep hear my voice, and I know them, and they follow me. ²⁸ I give them eternal life, and they will never perish, and no one will snatch them out of my hand. ²⁹ My Father, who has given them to me, is greater than all, and no one is able to snatch them out of the Father's hand. ³⁰ I and the Father are one."		

KEY WORDS	DEFINITIONS	CROSS REFERENCES

MAIN POINT(S)

APPLY

PRAY

day *four*

JOHN 10:31-42

READ	OBSERVE	INTERPRET
[31] The Jews picked up stones again to stone him. [32] Jesus answered them, "I have shown you many good works from the Father; for which of them are you going to stone me?" [33] The Jews answered him, "It is not for a good work that we are going to stone you but for blasphemy, because you, being a man, make yourself God." [34] Jesus answered them, "Is it not written in your Law, 'I said, you are gods'? [35] If he called them gods to whom the word of God came—and Scripture cannot be broken— [36] do you say of him whom the Father consecrated and sent into the world, 'You are blaspheming,' because I said, 'I am the Son of God'? [37] If I am not doing the works of my Father, then do not believe me; [38] but if I do them, even though you do not believe me, believe the works, that you may know and understand that the Father is in me and I am in the Father." [39] Again they sought to arrest him, but he escaped from their hands. [40] He went away again across the Jordan to the place where John had been baptizing at first, and there he remained. [41] And many came to him. And they said, "John did no sign, but everything that John said about this man was true." [42] And many believed in him there.		

KEY WORDS	DEFINITIONS	CROSS REFERENCES

MAIN POINT(S)	APPLY

PRAY

day *five*

JOHN 10 | REVIEW & DISCUSSION QUESTIONS

Summary:	Write out a favorite verse(s) from the passage, perhaps in your own words:
What is Jesus saying in the first five verses?	Explain how Jesus is "the door."
According to Jesus, what characteristics make a "Good Shepherd?"	How can "thieves and robbers" be recognized?

Have you ever been "duped" by a "thief or robber?" How do we guard against them? How do we guard against becoming one?	What benefits do the Good Shepherd's sheep enjoy?
What do you make of Jesus's statements in verses 34-35? What's His view of Scripture?	What are the reactions of the people? Had you been present to hear Jesus, what might you have thought? Looking back and reflecting, what are your thoughts concerning Jesus?
What evidence does Jesus provide for His identity? Is this enough? Why or why not?	Praise God for at least one truth from this week's study:

I GIVE THEM ETERNAL LIFE,
AND THEY WILL NEVER PERISH,
AND NO ONE WILL SNATCH
THEM OUT OF MY HAND.

JOHN 10:28

week *thirteen*

LESSON 12: JOHN 11

day *one*

READ

¹ Now a certain man was ill, Lazarus of Bethany, the village of Mary and her sister Martha. ² It was Mary who anointed the Lord with ointment and wiped his feet with her hair, whose brother Lazarus was ill. ³ So the sisters sent to him, saying, "Lord, he whom you love is ill." ⁴ But when Jesus heard it he said, "This illness does not lead to death. It is for the glory of God, so that the Son of God may be glorified through it." ⁵ Now Jesus loved Martha and her sister and Lazarus. ⁶ So, when he heard that Lazarus was ill, he stayed two days longer in the place where he was. ⁷ Then after this he said to the disciples, "Let us go to Judea again." ⁸ The disciples said to him, "Rabbi, the Jews were just now seeking to stone you, and are you going there again?" ⁹ Jesus answered, "Are there not twelve hours in the day? If anyone walks in the day, he does not stumble, because he sees the light of this world. ¹⁰ But if anyone walks in the night, he stumbles, because the light is not in him." ¹¹ After saying these things, he said to them, "Our friend Lazarus has fallen asleep, but I go to awaken him." ¹² The disciples said to him, "Lord, if he has fallen asleep, he will recover." ¹³ Now Jesus had spoken of his death, but they thought that he meant taking rest in sleep. ¹⁴ Then Jesus told them plainly, "Lazarus has died, ¹⁵ and for your sake I am glad that I was not there, so that you may believe. But let us go to him." ¹⁶ So Thomas, called the Twin, said to his fellow disciples, "Let us also go, that we may die with him."

OBSERVE

INTERPRET

KEY WORDS	DEFINITIONS	CROSS REFERENCES

MAIN POINT(S)	APPLY

PRAY

day *two*

JOHN 11:17-27

READ	OBSERVE	INTERPRET
¹⁷ Now when Jesus came, he found that Lazarus had already been in the tomb four days. ¹⁸ Bethany was near Jerusalem, about two miles off, ¹⁹ and many of the Jews had come to Martha and Mary to console them concerning their brother. ²⁰ So when Martha heard that Jesus was coming, she went and met him, but Mary remained seated in the house. ²¹ Martha said to Jesus, "Lord, if you had been here, my brother would not have died. ²² But even now I know that whatever you ask from God, God will give you." ²³ Jesus said to her, "Your brother will rise again." ²⁴ Martha said to him, "I know that he will rise again in the resurrection on the last day." ²⁵ Jesus said to her, "I am the resurrection and the life. Whoever believes in me, though he die, yet shall he live, ²⁶ and everyone who lives and believes in me shall never die. Do you believe this?" ²⁷ She said to him, "Yes, Lord; I believe that you are the Christ, the Son of God, who is coming into the world."		

KEY WORDS	DEFINITIONS	CROSS REFERENCES

MAIN POINT(S)	APPLY

PRAY

day *three*

READ

OBSERVE

28 When she had said this, she went and called her sister Mary, saying in private, "The Teacher is here and is calling for you." 29 And when she heard it, she rose quickly and went to him. 30 Now Jesus had not yet come into the village, but was still in the place where Martha had met him. 31 When the Jews who were with her in the house, consoling her, saw Mary rise quickly and go out, they followed her, supposing that she was going to the tomb to weep there. 32 Now when Mary came to where Jesus was and saw him, she fell at his feet, saying to him, "Lord, if you had been here, my brother would not have died." 33 When Jesus saw her weeping, and the Jews who had come with her also weeping, he was deeply moved in his spirit and greatly troubled. 34 And he said, "Where have you laid him?" They said to him, "Lord, come and see." 35 Jesus wept. 36 So the Jews said, "See how he loved him!" 37 But some of them said, "Could not he who opened the eyes of the blind man also have kept this man from dying?" 38 Then Jesus, deeply moved again, came to the tomb. It was a cave, and a stone lay against it. 39 Jesus said, "Take away the stone." Martha, the sister of the dead man, said to him, "Lord, by this time there will be an odor, for he has been dead four days." 40 Jesus said to her, "Did I not tell you that if you believed you would see the glory of God?" 41 So they took away the stone. And Jesus lifted up his eyes and said, "Father, I thank you that you have heard me. 42 I knew that you always hear me, but I said this on account of the people standing around, that they may believe that you sent me." 43 When he had said these things, he cried out with a loud voice, "Lazarus, come out." 44 The man who had died came out, his hands and feet bound with linen strips, and his face wrapped with a cloth. Jesus said to them, "Unbind him, and let him go."

INTERPRET

KEY WORDS	DEFINITIONS	CROSS REFERENCES

MAIN POINT(S)	APPLY

PRAY

day *four*

READ

⁴⁵ Many of the Jews therefore, who had come with Mary and had seen what he did, believed in him, ⁴⁶ but some of them went to the Pharisees and told them what Jesus had done. ⁴⁷ So the chief priests and the Pharisees gathered the council and said, "What are we to do? For this man performs many signs. ⁴⁸ If we let him go on like this, everyone will believe in him, and the Romans will come and take away both our place and our nation." ⁴⁹ But one of them, Caiaphas, who was high priest that year, said to them, "You know nothing at all. ⁵⁰ Nor do you understand that it is better for you that one man should die for the people, not that the whole nation should perish." ⁵¹ He did not say this of his own accord, but being high priest that year he prophesied that Jesus would die for the nation, ⁵² and not for the nation only, but also to gather into one the children of God who are scattered abroad. ⁵³ So from that day on they made plans to put him to death.

⁵⁴ Jesus therefore no longer walked openly among the Jews, but went from there to the region near the wilderness, to a town called Ephraim, and there he stayed with the disciples. ⁵⁵ Now the Passover of the Jews was at hand, and many went up from the country to Jerusalem before the Passover to purify themselves. ⁵⁶ They were looking for Jesus and saying to one another as they stood in the temple, "What do you think? That he will not come to the feast at all?" ⁵⁷ Now the chief priests and the Pharisees had given orders that if anyone knew where he was, he should let them know, so that they might arrest him.

OBSERVE

INTERPRET

KEY WORDS	DEFINITIONS	CROSS REFERENCES

MAIN POINT(S)

APPLY

PRAY

day *five*

JOHN 11 | REVIEW & DISCUSSION QUESTIONS

Summary:	Write out a favorite verse(s) from the passage, perhaps in your own words:
In the account of Jesus raising Lazarus from the dead, what popped out to you?	How does Jesus respond when He hears that Lazarus is sick? Why?
The disciples remind Jesus of the dangers in Jerusalem. What do you learn about Jesus from His response?	How might this apply to your own priorities?

This chapter offers another "I Am" statement (11:25-26). What is it and what is Jesus really asking Martha?

Verse 35 is the shortest verse in Scripture, yet incredibly poignant. What do you learn about Jesus from verses 33-35?

This is the last great "sign" recorded by John. What are the various reactions to Christ's miracle?

How is Caiaphus's statement (11:50) prophetic? Why are the Pharisees fearful?

What is your own reaction to this miracle? How might it apply to your own life today and in the future?

Praise God for at least one truth from this week's study:

JESUS WEPT.

JOHN 11:35

week *fourteen*

LESSON 13: JOHN 12

day *one*

JOHN 12:1-11

READ	OBSERVE	INTERPRET
¹ Six days before the Passover, Jesus therefore came to Bethany, where Lazarus was, whom Jesus had raised from the dead. ² So they gave a dinner for him there. Martha served, and Lazarus was one of those reclining with him at table. ³ Mary therefore took a pound of expensive ointment made from pure nard, and anointed the feet of Jesus and wiped his feet with her hair. The house was filled with the fragrance of the perfume. ⁴ But Judas Iscariot, one of his disciples (he who was about to betray him), said, ⁵ "Why was this ointment not sold for three hundred denarii and given to the poor?" ⁶ He said this, not because he cared about the poor, but because he was a thief, and having charge of the moneybag he used to help himself to what was put into it. ⁷ Jesus said, "Leave her alone, so that she may keep it for the day of my burial. ⁸ For the poor you always have with you, but you do not always have me." ⁹ When the large crowd of the Jews learned that Jesus was there, they came, not only on account of him but also to see Lazarus, whom he had raised from the dead. ¹⁰ So the chief priests made plans to put Lazarus to death as well, ¹¹ because on account of him many of the Jews were going away and believing in Jesus.		

KEY WORDS	DEFINITIONS	CROSS REFERENCES

MAIN POINT(S)

APPLY

PRAY

day *two*

READ	OBSERVE	INTERPRET
[12] The next day the large crowd that had come to the feast heard that Jesus was coming to Jerusalem. [13] So they took branches of palm trees and went out to meet him, crying out, "Hosanna! Blessed is he who comes in the name of the Lord, even the King of Israel!" [14] And Jesus found a young donkey and sat on it, just as it is written, [15] "Fear not, daughter of Zion; behold, your king is coming, sitting on a donkey's colt!" [16] His disciples did not understand these things at first, but when Jesus was glorified, then they remembered that these things had been written about him and had been done to him. [17] The crowd that had been with him when he called Lazarus out of the tomb and raised him from the dead continued to bear witness. [18] The reason why the crowd went to meet him was that they heard he had done this sign. [19] So the Pharisees said to one another, "You see that you are gaining nothing. Look, the world has gone after him."		

KEY WORDS	DEFINITIONS	CROSS REFERENCES

MAIN POINT(S)

APPLY

PRAY

day *three*

JOHN 12:20-36

READ

²⁰ Now among those who went up to worship at the feast were some Greeks. ²¹ So these came to Philip, who was from Bethsaida in Galilee, and asked him, "Sir, we wish to see Jesus." ²² Philip went and told Andrew; Andrew and Philip went and told Jesus. ²³ And Jesus answered them, "The hour has come for the Son of Man to be glorified. ²⁴ Truly, truly, I say to you, unless a grain of wheat falls into the earth and dies, it remains alone; but if it dies, it bears much fruit. ²⁵ Whoever loves his life loses it, and whoever hates his life in this world will keep it for eternal life. ²⁶ If anyone serves me, he must follow me; and where I am, there will my servant be also. If anyone serves me, the Father will honor him.

²⁷ "Now is my soul troubled. And what shall I say? 'Father, save me from this hour'? But for this purpose I have come to this hour. ²⁸ Father, glorify your name." Then a voice came from heaven: "I have glorified it, and I will glorify it again." ²⁹ The crowd that stood there and heard it said that it had thundered. Others said, "An angel has spoken to him." ³⁰ Jesus answered, "This voice has come for your sake, not mine. ³¹ Now is the judgment of this world; now will the ruler of this world be cast out. ³² And I, when I am lifted up from the earth, will draw all people to myself." ³³ He said this to show by what kind of death he was going to die. ³⁴ So the crowd answered him, "We have heard from the Law that the Christ remains forever. How can you say that the Son of Man must be lifted up? Who is this Son of Man?" ³⁵ So Jesus said to them, "The light is among you for a little while longer. Walk while you have the light, lest darkness overtake you. The one who walks in the darkness does not know where he is going. ³⁶ While you have the light, believe in the light, that you may become sons of light."

OBSERVE

INTERPRET

KEY WORDS	DEFINITIONS	CROSS REFERENCES

MAIN POINT(S)

APPLY

PRAY

day *four*

READ

When Jesus had said these things, he departed and hid himself from them. [37] Though he had done so many signs before them, they still did not believe in him, [38] so that the word spoken by the prophet Isaiah might be fulfilled:

"Lord, who has believed what he heard from us,
    and to whom has the arm of the Lord been revealed?"

[39] Therefore they could not believe. For again Isaiah said,

[40] "He has blinded their eyes
    and hardened their heart,
lest they see with their eyes,
    and understand with their heart, and turn,
    and I would heal them."

[41] Isaiah said these things because he saw his glory and spoke of him. [42] Nevertheless, many even of the authorities believed in him, but for fear of the Pharisees they did not confess it, so that they would not be put out of the synagogue; [43] for they loved the glory that comes from man more than the glory that comes from God.

[44] And Jesus cried out and said, "Whoever believes in me, believes not in me but in him who sent me. [45] And whoever sees me sees him who sent me. [46] I have come into the world as light, so that whoever believes in me may not remain in darkness. [47] If anyone hears my words and does not keep them, I do not judge him; for I did not come to judge the world but to save the world. [48] The one who rejects me and does not receive my words has a judge; the word that I have spoken will judge him on the last day. [49] For I have not spoken on my own authority, but the Father who sent me has himself given me a commandment—what to say and what to speak. [50] And I know that his commandment is eternal life. What I say, therefore, I say as the Father has told me."

OBSERVE

INTERPRET

KEY WORDS	DEFINITIONS	CROSS REFERENCES

MAIN POINT(S)	APPLY

PRAY

day *five*

Summary:	Write out a favorite verse(s) from the passage, perhaps in your own words:
What are the different ways Martha, Lazarus, and Mary interact with Jesus?	What do you think motivated Mary? What is scandalous about her behavior? Thoughts?
What is the complaint of Judas?	With which dinner character do you most identify: Martha, Lazarus, Mary, or Judas? Why?

Mary shares her devotion in a costly way. What would a costly act look like for you today?	Please share your thoughts concerning verses 12-19. What does John want us to know and take to heart?
Contrast the desires of the Pharisees with those of the Greeks? Why might John include these accounts side by side?	Put into your own words the truths that Jesus teaches concerning His death. (12:23-26)
Contrast the light and dark according to Christ's teaching. Why would the religious leaders not speak up about their faith? How is this relevant today?	Praise God for at least one truth from this week's study:

I HAVE COME INTO
THE WORLD AS LIGHT, SO
THAT WHOEVER BELIEVES
IN ME MAY NOT REMAIN
IN DARKNESS.

JOHN 12:46

week *fifteen*

LESSON 14: JOHN 13

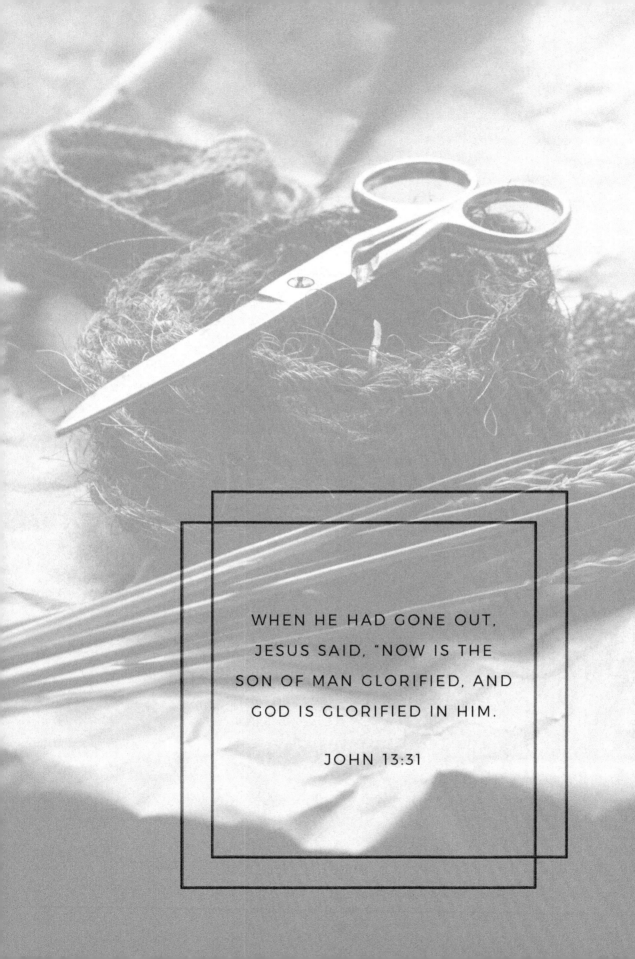

WHEN HE HAD GONE OUT,
JESUS SAID, "NOW IS THE
SON OF MAN GLORIFIED, AND
GOD IS GLORIFIED IN HIM.

JOHN 13:31

day *one*

READ

¹ Now before the Feast of the Passover, when Jesus knew that his hour had come to depart out of this world to the Father, having loved his own who were in the world, he loved them to the end. ² During supper, when the devil had already put it into the heart of Judas Iscariot, Simon's son, to betray him, ³ Jesus, knowing that the Father had given all things into his hands, and that he had come from God and was going back to God, ⁴ rose from supper. He laid aside his outer garments, and taking a towel, tied it around his waist. ⁵ Then he poured water into a basin and began to wash the disciples' feet and to wipe them with the towel that was wrapped around him. ⁶ He came to Simon Peter, who said to him, "Lord, do you wash my feet?" ⁷ Jesus answered him, "What I am doing you do not understand now, but afterward you will understand." ⁸ Peter said to him, "You shall never wash my feet." Jesus answered him, "If I do not wash you, you have no share with me." ⁹ Simon Peter said to him, "Lord, not my feet only but also my hands and my head!" ¹⁰ Jesus said to him, "The one who has bathed does not need to wash, except for his feet, but is completely clean. And you are clean, but not every one of you." ¹¹ For he knew who was to betray him; that was why he said, "Not all of you are clean."

¹² When he had washed their feet and put on his outer garments and resumed his place, he said to them, "Do you understand what I have done to you? ¹³ You call me Teacher and Lord, and you are right, for so I am. ¹⁴ If I then, your Lord and Teacher, have washed your feet, you also ought to wash one another's feet. ¹⁵ For I have given you an example, that you also should do just as I have done to you. ¹⁶ Truly, truly, I say to you, a servant is not greater than his master, nor is a messenger greater than the one who sent him. ¹⁷ If you know these things, blessed are you if you do them. ¹⁸ I am not speaking of all of you; I know whom I have chosen. But the Scripture will be fulfilled, 'He who ate my bread has lifted his heel against me.' ¹⁹ I am telling you this now, before it takes place, that when it does take place you may believe that I am he.

²⁰ Truly, truly, I say to you, whoever receives the one I send receives me, and whoever receives me receives the one who sent me."

OBSERVE	INTERPRET

KEY WORDS	DEFINITIONS	CROSS REFERENCES

MAIN POINT(S)

APPLY

PRAY

day *two*

READ	OBSERVE	INTERPRET
21 After saying these things, Jesus was troubled in his spirit, and testified, "Truly, truly, I say to you, one of you will betray me." 22 The disciples looked at one another, uncertain of whom he spoke. 23 One of his disciples, whom Jesus loved, was reclining at table at Jesus' side, 24 so Simon Peter motioned to him to ask Jesus of whom he was speaking. 25 So that disciple, leaning back against Jesus, said to him, "Lord, who is it?" 26 Jesus answered, "It is he to whom I will give this morsel of bread when I have dipped it." So when he had dipped the morsel, he gave it to Judas, the son of Simon Iscariot. 27 Then after he had taken the morsel, Satan entered into him. Jesus said to him, "What you are going to do, do quickly." 28 Now no one at the table knew why he said this to him. 29 Some thought that, because Judas had the moneybag, Jesus was telling him, "Buy what we need for the feast," or that he should give something to the poor. 30 So, after receiving the morsel of bread, he immediately went out. And it was night.		

KEY WORDS	DEFINITIONS	CROSS REFERENCES

MAIN POINT(S)

APPLY

PRAY

day *three*

READ	OBSERVE	INTERPRET
[31] When he had gone out, Jesus said, "Now is the Son of Man glorified, and God is glorified in him. [32] If God is glorified in him, God will also glorify him in himself, and glorify him at once. [33] Little children, yet a little while I am with you. You will seek me, and just as I said to the Jews, so now I also say to you, 'Where I am going you cannot come.' [34] A new commandment I give to you, that you love one another: just as I have loved you, you also are to love one another. [35] By this all people will know that you are my disciples, if you have love for one another."		

KEY WORDS	DEFINITIONS	CROSS REFERENCES

MAIN POINT(S)

APPLY

PRAY

day *four*

READ	OBSERVE	INTERPRET
[36] Simon Peter said to him, "Lord, where are you going?" Jesus answered him, "Where I am going you cannot follow me now, but you will follow afterward." [37] Peter said to him, "Lord, why can I not follow you now? I will lay down my life for you." [38] Jesus answered, "Will you lay down your life for me? Truly, truly, I say to you, the rooster will not crow till you have denied me three times.		

KEY WORDS	DEFINITIONS	CROSS REFERENCES

MAIN POINT(S)

APPLY

PRAY

day *five*

JOHN 13 | REVIEW & DISCUSSION QUESTIONS

Summary:	Write out a favorite verse(s) from the passage, perhaps in your own words:
Describe Jesus in verses 1-5. What do you learn by His example?	What is Peter's initial response when Jesus wants to wash his feet? What do you learn about Peter?
What does Jesus want His disciples to learn from the foot-washing? (13:8-10, 13:12-17)	In what ways do you need Jesus to wash your feet today?

How does Jesus's example and teaching challenge you in serving Him and serving others?	Describe Christ in verse 21. How might His openness to authentic love relationships that include both friendship and hurt be an example for our own relationships?
How does Jesus reveal His betrayer? Why reveal him in such a discrete way?	What new commandment does Jesus give and why is this so crucial for Christians?
How can Christians loving one another lead to effective evangelism? What is one practical way you could love a sister in Christ this week?	Praise God for at least one truth from this week's study:

A NEW COMMANDMENT I
GIVE TO YOU, THAT YOU
LOVE ONE ANOTHER: JUST
AS I HAVE LOVED YOU,
YOU ALSO ARE TO
LOVE ONE ANOTHER.

JOHN 13:34

week *sixteen*

LESSON 15: JOHN 14

day *one*

JOHN 14:1-7

READ	OBSERVE	INTERPRET
[1] "Let not your hearts be troubled. Believe in God; believe also in me. [2] In my Father's house are many rooms. If it were not so, would I have told you that I go to prepare a place for you? [3] And if I go and prepare a place for you, I will come again and will take you to myself, that where I am you may be also. [4] And you know the way to where I am going." [5] Thomas said to him, "Lord, we do not know where you are going. How can we know the way?" [6] Jesus said to him, "I am the way, and the truth, and the life. No one comes to the Father except through me. [7] If you had known me, you would have known my Father also. From now on you do know him and have seen him."		

KEY WORDS	DEFINITIONS	CROSS REFERENCES

MAIN POINT(S)

APPLY

PRAY

day *two*

JOHN 14:8-14

READ	OBSERVE	INTERPRET
[8] Philip said to him, "Lord, show us the Father, and it is enough for us." [9] Jesus said to him, "Have I been with you so long, and you still do not know me, Philip? Whoever has seen me has seen the Father. How can you say, 'Show us the Father'? [10] Do you not believe that I am in the Father and the Father is in me? The words that I say to you I do not speak on my own authority, but the Father who dwells in me does his works. [11] Believe me that I am in the Father and the Father is in me, or else believe on account of the works themselves. [12] "Truly, truly, I say to you, whoever believes in me will also do the works that I do; and greater works than these will he do, because I am going to the Father. [13] Whatever you ask in my name, this I will do, that the Father may be glorified in the Son. [14] If you ask me anything in my name, I will do it.		

KEY WORDS	DEFINITIONS	CROSS REFERENCES

MAIN POINT(S)

APPLY

PRAY

day *three*

READ	OBSERVE	INTERPRET
[15] "If you love me, you will keep my commandments. [16] And I will ask the Father, and he will give you another Helper, to be with you forever, [17] even the Spirit of truth, whom the world cannot receive, because it neither sees him nor knows him. You know him, for he dwells with you and will be in you. [18] "I will not leave you as orphans; I will come to you. [19] Yet a little while and the world will see me no more, but you will see me. Because I live, you also will live. [20] In that day you will know that I am in my Father, and you in me, and I in you. [21] Whoever has my commandments and keeps them, he it is who loves me. And he who loves me will be loved by my Father, and I will love him and manifest myself to him." [22] Judas (not Iscariot) said to him, "Lord, how is it that you will manifest yourself to us, and not to the world?" [23] Jesus answered him, "If anyone loves me, he will keep my word, and my Father will love him, and we will come to him and make our home with him. [24] Whoever does not love me does not keep my words. And the word that you hear is not mine but the Father's who sent me.		

KEY WORDS	DEFINITIONS	CROSS REFERENCES

MAIN POINT(S)

APPLY

PRAY

day *four*

READ	OBSERVE	INTERPRET
25 "These things I have spoken to you while I am still with you. 26 But the Helper, the Holy Spirit, whom the Father will send in my name, he will teach you all things and bring to your remembrance all that I have said to you. 27 Peace I leave with you; my peace I give to you. Not as the world gives do I give to you. Let not your hearts be troubled, neither let them be afraid. 28 You heard me say to you, 'I am going away, and I will come to you.' If you loved me, you would have rejoiced, because I am going to the Father, for the Father is greater than I. 29 And now I have told you before it takes place, so that when it does take place you may believe. 30 I will no longer talk much with you, for the ruler of this world is coming. He has no claim on me, 31 but I do as the Father has commanded me, so that the world may know that I love the Father. Rise, let us go from here.		

KEY WORDS	DEFINITIONS	CROSS REFERENCES

MAIN POINT(S)	APPLY

PRAY

day *five*

JOHN 14 | REVIEW & DISCUSSION QUESTIONS

Summary:	Write out a favorite verse(s) from the passage, perhaps in your own words:
In this chapter, we see Jesus privately ministering to His disciples. Why might He reassure them now?	What reassurances does He give them?
What bold statement does He make in regards to Himself? (14:6)	Why is this statement "uncomfortable"? How would you respond to one who claims Jesus is *a* way rather than *the* way?

How does the hope of heaven encourage you? (14:1-3) How does that hope affect how you live now?	What insights do you gain concerning the importance of obedience? Are there any commands of Christ that are needing attention in your life? How can you better show your love?
Jesus promises to send a helper. Who is this and what do you learn about Him?	What do you learn about prayer from this chapter? (14:13-14)
What do you learn about peace from this chapter? Have you experienced the peace to which Christ refers? (14:27)	Praise God for at least one truth from this week's study:

I AM THE WAY, AND THE
TRUTH, AND THE LIFE.
NO ONE COMES TO THE FATHER
EXCEPT THROUGH ME.

JOHN 14:6

week *seventeen*

LESSON 16: JOHN 15

day *one*

READ	OBSERVE	INTERPRET
[1] "I am the true vine, and my Father is the vinedresser. [2] Every branch in me that does not bear fruit he takes away, and every branch that does bear fruit he prunes, that it may bear more fruit. [3] Already you are clean because of the word that I have spoken to you. [4] Abide in me, and I in you. As the branch cannot bear fruit by itself, unless it abides in the vine, neither can you, unless you abide in me. [5] I am the vine; you are the branches. Whoever abides in me and I in him, he it is that bears much fruit, for apart from me you can do nothing. [6] If anyone does not abide in me he is thrown away like a branch and withers; and the branches are gathered, thrown into the fire, and burned. [7] If you abide in me, and my words abide in you, ask whatever you wish, and it will be done for you.		

KEY WORDS	DEFINITIONS	CROSS REFERENCES

MAIN POINT(S)

APPLY

PRAY

day *two*

JOHN 15:8-11

READ	OBSERVE	INTERPRET
[8] By this my Father is glorified, that you bear much fruit and so prove to be my disciples. [9] As the Father has loved me, so have I loved you. Abide in my love. [10] If you keep my commandments, you will abide in my love, just as I have kept my Father's commandments and abide in his love. [11] These things I have spoken to you, that my joy may be in you, and that your joy may be full.		

KEY WORDS	DEFINITIONS	CROSS REFERENCES

MAIN POINT(S)

APPLY

PRAY

day *three*

READ	OBSERVE	INTERPRET
¹² "This is my commandment, that you love one another as I have loved you. ¹³ Greater love has no one than this, that someone lay down his life for his friends. ¹⁴ You are my friends if you do what I command you. ¹⁵ No longer do I call you servants, for the servant does not know what his master is doing; but I have called you friends, for all that I have heard from my Father I have made known to you. ¹⁶ You did not choose me, but I chose you and appointed you that you should go and bear fruit and that your fruit should abide, so that whatever you ask the Father in my name, he may give it to you. ¹⁷ These things I command you, so that you will love one another.		

KEY WORDS	DEFINITIONS	CROSS REFERENCES

MAIN POINT(S)	APPLY

PRAY

day *four*

READ	OBSERVE	INTERPRET
¹⁸ "If the world hates you, know that it has hated me before it hated you. ¹⁹ If you were of the world, the world would love you as its own; but because you are not of the world, but I chose you out of the world, therefore the world hates you. ²⁰ Remember the word that I said to you: 'A servant is not greater than his master.' If they persecuted me, they will also persecute you. If they kept my word, they will also keep yours. ²¹ But all these things they will do to you on account of my name, because they do not know him who sent me. ²² If I had not come and spoken to them, they would not have been guilty of sin, but now they have no excuse for their sin. ²³ Whoever hates me hates my Father also. ²⁴ If I had not done among them the works that no one else did, they would not be guilty of sin, but now they have seen and hated both me and my Father. ²⁵ But the word that is written in their Law must be fulfilled: 'They hated me without a cause.' ²⁶ "But when the Helper comes, whom I will send to you from the Father, the Spirit of truth, who proceeds from the Father, he will bear witness about me. ²⁷ And you also will bear witness, because you have been with me from the beginning.		

KEY WORDS	DEFINITIONS	CROSS REFERENCES

MAIN POINT(S)

APPLY

PRAY

day *five*

JOHN 15 | REVIEW & DISCUSSION QUESTIONS

Summary:	Write out a favorite verse(s) from the passage, perhaps in your own words:
Define: true vine, vinedresser, branch, prune, and abide according to Jesus.	According to verses 2, 5-8, and 16, what is our purpose? What does that mean?
Apart from the vine, a branch is dead. What practical ways can we abide in Christ?	Describe one way you have been "pruned."

According to Jesus, what is the highest form of love? (15:13)	What are practical ways that we can sacrificially love one another?
Jesus called his disciples "friends." (15:14-15) Why is this significant? How does this make you feel?	According to Jesus, why does the world hate His followers? (15:19-21) Describe what this means to you.
What comfort does Jesus offer to His disciples? (15:26)	Praise God for at least one truth from this week's study:

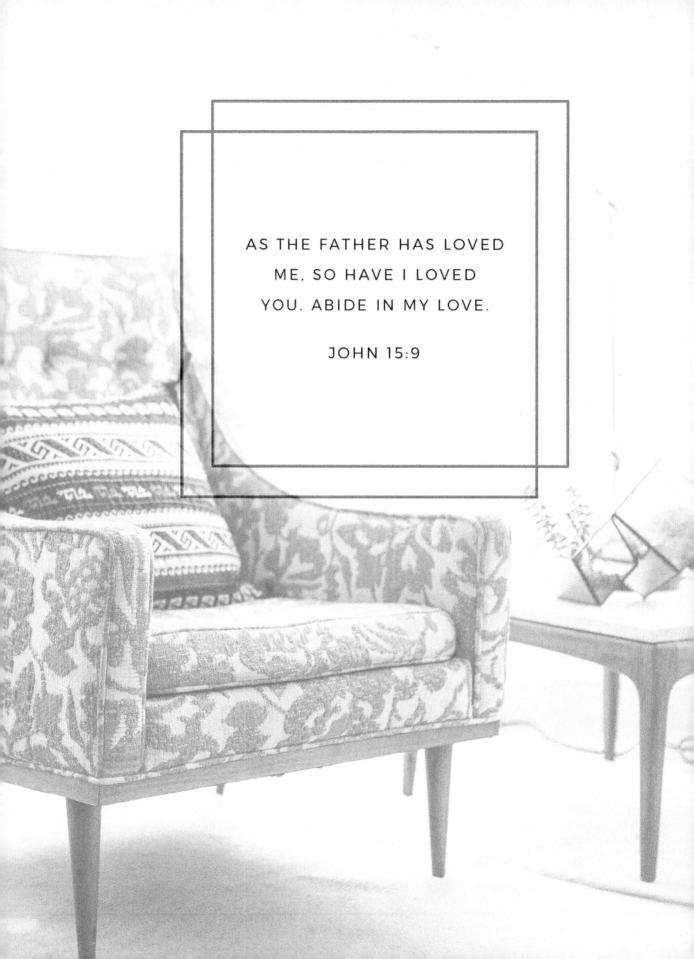

AS THE FATHER HAS LOVED
ME, SO HAVE I LOVED
YOU. ABIDE IN MY LOVE.

JOHN 15:9

week *eighteen*

LESSON 17: JOHN 16

day *one*

JOHN 16:1-11

READ	OBSERVE	INTERPRET
[1] "I have said all these things to you to keep you from falling away. [2] They will put you out of the synagogues. Indeed, the hour is coming when whoever kills you will think he is offering service to God. [3] And they will do these things because they have not known the Father, nor me. [4] But I have said these things to you, that when their hour comes you may remember that I told them to you. "I did not say these things to you from the beginning, because I was with you. [5] But now I am going to him who sent me, and none of you asks me, 'Where are you going?' [6] But because I have said these things to you, sorrow has filled your heart. [7] Nevertheless, I tell you the truth: it is to your advantage that I go away, for if I do not go away, the Helper will not come to you. But if I go, I will send him to you. [8] And when he comes, he will convict the world concerning sin and righteousness and judgment: [9] concerning sin, because they do not believe in me; [10] concerning righteousness, because I go to the Father, and you will see me no longer; [11] concerning judgment, because the ruler of this world is judged.		

KEY WORDS	DEFINITIONS	CROSS REFERENCES

MAIN POINT(S)

APPLY

PRAY

day *two*

JOHN 16:12-15

READ	OBSERVE	INTERPRET
[12] "I still have many things to say to you, but you cannot bear them now. [13] When the Spirit of truth comes, he will guide you into all the truth, for he will not speak on his own authority, but whatever he hears he will speak, and he will declare to you the things that are to come. [14] He will glorify me, for he will take what is mine and declare it to you. [15] All that the Father has is mine; therefore I said that he will take what is mine and declare it to you.		

KEY WORDS	DEFINITIONS	CROSS REFERENCES

MAIN POINT(S)

APPLY

PRAY

day *three*

JOHN 16:16-24

READ	OBSERVE	INTERPRET
[16] "A little while, and you will see me no longer; and again a little while, and you will see me." [17] So some of his disciples said to one another, "What is this that he says to us, 'A little while, and you will not see me, and again a little while, and you will see me'; and, 'because I am going to the Father'?" [18] So they were saying, "What does he mean by 'a little while'? We do not know what he is talking about." [19] Jesus knew that they wanted to ask him, so he said to them, "Is this what you are asking yourselves, what I meant by saying, 'A little while and you will not see me, and again a little while and you will see me'? [20] Truly, truly, I say to you, you will weep and lament, but the world will rejoice. You will be sorrowful, but your sorrow will turn into joy. [21] When a woman is giving birth, she has sorrow because her hour has come, but when she has delivered the baby, she no longer remembers the anguish, for joy that a human being has been born into the world. [22] So also you have sorrow now, but I will see you again, and your hearts will rejoice, and no one will take your joy from you. [23] In that day you will ask nothing of me. Truly, truly, I say to you, whatever you ask of the Father in my name, he will give it to you. [24] Until now you have asked nothing in my name. Ask, and you will receive, that your joy may be full.		

KEY WORDS	DEFINITIONS	CROSS REFERENCES

MAIN POINT(S)	APPLY

PRAY

day *four*

JOHN 16:25-33

READ	OBSERVE	INTERPRET
25 "I have said these things to you in figures of speech. The hour is coming when I will no longer speak to you in figures of speech but will tell you plainly about the Father. 26 In that day you will ask in my name, and I do not say to you that I will ask the Father on your behalf; 27 for the Father himself loves you, because you have loved me and have believed that I came from God. 28 I came from the Father and have come into the world, and now I am leaving the world and going to the Father." 29 His disciples said, "Ah, now you are speaking plainly and not using figurative speech! 30 Now we know that you know all things and do not need anyone to question you; this is why we believe that you came from God." 31 Jesus answered them, "Do you now believe? 32 Behold, the hour is coming, indeed it has come, when you will be scattered, each to his own home, and will leave me alone. Yet I am not alone, for the Father is with me. 33 I have said these things to you, that in me you may have peace. In the world you will have tribulation. But take heart; I have overcome the world."		

KEY WORDS	DEFINITIONS	CROSS REFERENCES

MAIN POINT(S)

APPLY

PRAY

day *five*

JOHN 16 | REVIEW & DISCUSSION QUESTIONS

Summary:	Write out a favorite verse(s) from the passage, perhaps in your own words:
Why does Jesus provide the disciple with a heads-up concerning the upcoming "hour?" (16:1-4)	How does the Holy Spirit convict the world of sin? (16:8-11)
How does the Holy Spirit lead believers into truth? (16:13-15)	In what ways have you experienced the Holy Spirit leading you to better know Jesus?

Verse 20 provides another "truly, truly" statement. What analogy is used and how is this appropriate?	Verse 23 contains yet another "truly, truly" statement. Please explain it in your own words.
Describe Christ's relationship with the Father. (16:25-32)	John 16:33 is worth memorizing! How do Christ's words differ from the world's "Don't worry, be happy" statement?
How do Christ's words encourage you to stand firm in the midst of trouble today?	Praise God for at least one truth from this week's study:

IN THE WORLD YOU WILL
HAVE TRIBULATION.
BUT TAKE HEART; I HAVE
OVERCOME THE WORLD.

JOHN 16:33

week *nineteen*

LESSON 18: JOHN 17

day *one*

JOHN 17:1-5

READ	OBSERVE	INTERPRET
[1] When Jesus had spoken these words, he lifted up his eyes to heaven, and said, "Father, the hour has come; glorify your Son that the Son may glorify you, [2] since you have given him authority over all flesh, to give eternal life to all whom you have given him. [3] And this is eternal life, that they know you, the only true God, and Jesus Christ whom you have sent. [4] I glorified you on earth, having accomplished the work that you gave me to do. [5] And now, Father, glorify me in your own presence with the glory that I had with you before the world existed.		

KEY WORDS	DEFINITIONS	CROSS REFERENCES

MAIN POINT(S)

APPLY

PRAY

day *two*

JOHN 17:6-12

READ	OBSERVE	INTERPRET
6 "I have manifested your name to the people whom you gave me out of the world. Yours they were, and you gave them to me, and they have kept your word. 7 Now they know that everything that you have given me is from you. 8 For I have given them the words that you gave me, and they have received them and have come to know in truth that I came from you; and they have believed that you sent me. 9 I am praying for them. I am not praying for the world but for those whom you have given me, for they are yours. 10 All mine are yours, and yours are mine, and I am glorified in them. 11 And I am no longer in the world, but they are in the world, and I am coming to you. Holy Father, keep them in your name, which you have given me, that they may be one, even as we are one. 12 While I was with them, I kept them in your name, which you have given me. I have guarded them, and not one of them has been lost except the son of destruction, that the Scripture might be fulfilled.		

KEY WORDS	DEFINITIONS	CROSS REFERENCES

MAIN POINT(S)

APPLY

PRAY

day *three*

READ	OBSERVE	INTERPRET
¹³ But now I am coming to you, and these things I speak in the world, that they may have my joy fulfilled in themselves. ¹⁴ I have given them your word, and the world has hated them because they are not of the world, just as I am not of the world. ¹⁵ I do not ask that you take them out of the world, but that you keep them from the evil one. ¹⁶ They are not of the world, just as I am not of the world. ¹⁷ Sanctify them in the truth; your word is truth. ¹⁸ As you sent me into the world, so I have sent them into the world. ¹⁹ And for their sake I consecrate myself, that they also may be sanctified in truth.		

KEY WORDS	DEFINITIONS	CROSS REFERENCES

MAIN POINT(S)

APPLY

PRAY

day *four*

JOHN 17:20-26

READ	OBSERVE	INTERPRET
20 "I do not ask for these only, but also for those who will believe in me through their word, 21 that they may all be one, just as you, Father, are in me, and I in you, that they also may be in us, so that the world may believe that you have sent me. 22 The glory that you have given me I have given to them, that they may be one even as we are one, 23 I in them and you in me, that they may become perfectly one, so that the world may know that you sent me and loved them even as you loved me. 24 Father, I desire that they also, whom you have given me, may be with me where I am, to see my glory that you have given me because you loved me before the foundation of the world. 25 O righteous Father, even though the world does not know you, I know you, and these know that you have sent me. 26 I made known to them your name, and I will continue to make it known, that the love with which you have loved me may be in them, and I in them."		

KEY WORDS	DEFINITIONS	CROSS REFERENCES

MAIN POINT(S)

APPLY

PRAY

day *five*

JOHN 17 | REVIEW & DISCUSSION QUESTIONS

Summary:	Write out a favorite verse(s) from the passage, perhaps in your own words:
Christ prays after speaking about what things (17:1)? Who does He pray for in verses 1-5? What does He celebrate and what does He request?	What has the Father given the Son? Is there anything else you notice concerning their relationship?
Who does Jesus pray for in verses 6-19? What does He celebrate and what does He request?	Concerning His disciples, what are Jesus's specific concerns?

Why doesn't Jesus take His disciples out of the world?	Who does Jesus pray for in verses 20-26? What does He celebrate and what does He request?
Why is unity amongst believers, Jesus and the Father so important? How have we failed and succeeded in attaining unity?	What can we do to facilitate unity within our church today?
How do we grow in unity with Christ and the Father?	Praise God for at least one truth from this week's study:

AND THIS IS ETERNAL LIFE,
THAT THEY KNOW YOU,
THE ONLY TRUE GOD,
AND JESUS CHRIST
WHOM YOU HAVE SENT.

JOHN 17:3

week *twenty*

LESSON 19: JOHN 18

day *one*

JOHN 18:1-14

READ

¹ When Jesus had spoken these words, he went out with his disciples across the brook Kidron, where there was a garden, which he and his disciples entered. ² Now Judas, who betrayed him, also knew the place, for Jesus often met there with his disciples. ³ So Judas, having procured a band of soldiers and some officers from the chief priests and the Pharisees, went there with lanterns and torches and weapons. ⁴ Then Jesus, knowing all that would happen to him, came forward and said to them, "Whom do you seek?" ⁵ They answered him, "Jesus of Nazareth." Jesus said to them, "I am he." Judas, who betrayed him, was standing with them. ⁶ When Jesus said to them, "I am he," they drew back and fell to the ground. ⁷ So he asked them again, "Whom do you seek?" And they said, "Jesus of Nazareth." ⁸ Jesus answered, "I told you that I am he. So, if you seek me, let these men go." ⁹ This was to fulfill the word that he had spoken: "Of those whom you gave me I have lost not one."

¹⁰ Then Simon Peter, having a sword, drew it and struck the high priest's servant and cut off his right ear. (The servant's name was Malchus.) ¹¹ So Jesus said to Peter, "Put your sword into its sheath; shall I not drink the cup that the Father has given me?"

¹² So the band of soldiers and their captain and the officers of the Jews arrested Jesus and bound him. ¹³ First they led him to Annas, for he was the father-in-law of Caiaphas, who was high priest that year. ¹⁴ It was Caiaphas who had advised the Jews that it would be expedient that one man should die for the people.

OBSERVE

INTERPRET

KEY WORDS

DEFINITIONS

CROSS REFERENCES

MAIN POINT(S)

APPLY

PRAY

day *two*

JOHN 18:15-27

READ

15 Simon Peter followed Jesus, and so did another disciple. Since that disciple was known to the high priest,
he entered with Jesus into the courtyard of the high
priest, 16 but Peter stood outside at the door. So the other
disciple, who was known to the high priest, went out and
spoke to the servant girl who kept watch at the door, and
brought Peter in. 17 The servant girl at the door said to
Peter, "You also are not one of this man's disciples, are
you?" He said, "I am not." 18 Now the servants and officers had made a charcoal fire, because it was cold, and
they were standing and warming themselves. Peter also
was with them, standing and warming himself.

19 The high priest then questioned Jesus about his disciples and his teaching. 20 Jesus answered him, "I have
spoken openly to the world. I have always taught in
synagogues and in the temple, where all Jews come together. I have said nothing in secret. 21 Why do you ask
me? Ask those who have heard me what I said to them;
they know what I said." 22 When he had said these
things, one of the officers standing by struck Jesus with
his hand, saying, "Is that how you answer the high
priest?" 23 Jesus answered him, "If what I said is wrong,
bear witness about the wrong; but if what I said is right,
why do you strike me?" 24 Annas then sent him bound to
Caiaphas the high priest.

25 Now Simon Peter was standing and warming himself.
So they said to him, "You also are not one of his disciples, are you?" He denied it and said, "I am not." 26 One
of the servants of the high priest, a relative of the man
whose ear Peter had cut off, asked, "Did I not see you in
the garden with him?" 27 Peter again denied it, and at
once a rooster crowed.

OBSERVE

INTERPRET

KEY WORDS	DEFINITIONS	CROSS REFERENCES

MAIN POINT(S)	APPLY

PRAY

day *three*

JOHN 18:28-32

READ	OBSERVE	INTERPRET
²⁸ Then they led Jesus from the house of Caiaphas to the governor's headquarters. It was early morning. They themselves did not enter the governor's headquarters, so that they would not be defiled, but could eat the Passover. ²⁹ So Pilate went outside to them and said, "What accusation do you bring against this man?" ³⁰ They answered him, "If this man were not doing evil, we would not have delivered him over to you." ³¹ Pilate said to them, "Take him yourselves and judge him by your own law." The Jews said to him, "It is not lawful for us to put anyone to death." ³² This was to fulfill the word that Jesus had spoken to show by what kind of death he was going to die.		

KEY WORDS	DEFINITIONS	CROSS REFERENCES

MAIN POINT(S)

APPLY

PRAY

day *four*

READ	OBSERVE	INTERPRET
³³ So Pilate entered his headquarters again and called Jesus and said to him, "Are you the King of the Jews?" ³⁴ Jesus answered, "Do you say this of your own accord, or did others say it to you about me?" ³⁵ Pilate answered, "Am I a Jew? Your own nation and the chief priests have delivered you over to me. What have you done?" ³⁶ Jesus answered, "My kingdom is not of this world. If my kingdom were of this world, my servants would have been fighting, that I might not be delivered over to the Jews. But my kingdom is not from the world." ³⁷ Then Pilate said to him, "So you are a king?" Jesus answered, "You say that I am a king. For this purpose I was born and for this purpose I have come into the world—to bear witness to the truth. Everyone who is of the truth listens to my voice." ³⁸ Pilate said to him, "What is truth?" After he had said this, he went back outside to the Jews and told them, "I find no guilt in him. ³⁹ But you have a custom that I should release one man for you at the Passover. So do you want me to release to you the King of the Jews?" ⁴⁰ They cried out again, "Not this man, but Barabbas!" Now Barabbas was a robber.		

KEY WORDS	DEFINITIONS	CROSS REFERENCES

MAIN POINT(S)	APPLY

PRAY

day *five*

Summary:	Write out a favorite verse(s) from the passage, perhaps in your own words:
What is significant about Jesus's response of "I am he" in verses 5, 6, and 8?	Why do you think the crowd responded as they did to "I am he," and why would John record this detail?
What do you learn about Peter in this chapter? Are you like him in any way?	What do you learn about the chief priests and their priorities? Are you like them in any specific way?

In verse 36, Jesus says, "My kingdom is not of this world." What does He mean? Are there implications for how you prioritize life?

How does Jesus respond to Pilate's question, "Are you the king of the Jews?"

What do Pilate's words and actions say about him? Do you recognize yourself in any way?

Jesus and Pilate have a discussion concerning truth. What does each mean and how is this relevant to our world today?

How can Jesus's attitude and behavior throughout the arrest and trial process provide an example for you to follow?

Praise God for at least one truth from this week's study:

FOR THIS PURPOSE
I WAS BORN AND FOR THIS
PURPOSE I HAVE COME
INTO THE WORLD—TO BEAR
WITNESS TO THE TRUTH.

JOHN 18:37

week *twenty-one*

LESSON 20: JOHN 19

day *one*

READ

¹ Then Pilate took Jesus and flogged him. ² And the soldiers twisted together a crown of thorns and put it on his head and arrayed him in a purple robe. ³ They came up to him, saying, "Hail, King of the Jews!" and struck him with their hands. ⁴ Pilate went out again and said to them, "See, I am bringing him out to you that you may know that I find no guilt in him." ⁵ So Jesus came out, wearing the crown of thorns and the purple robe. Pilate said to them, "Behold the man!" ⁶ When the chief priests and the officers saw him, they cried out, "Crucify him, crucify him!" Pilate said to them, "Take him yourselves and crucify him, for I find no guilt in him." ⁷ The Jews answered him, "We have a law, and according to that law he ought to die because he has made himself the Son of God." ⁸ When Pilate heard this statement, he was even more afraid. ⁹ He entered his headquarters again and said to Jesus, "Where are you from?" But Jesus gave him no answer. ¹⁰ So Pilate said to him, "You will not speak to me? Do you not know that I have authority to release you and authority to crucify you?" ¹¹ Jesus answered him, "You would have no authority over me at all unless it had been given you from above. Therefore he who delivered me over to you has the greater sin."

¹² From then on Pilate sought to release him, but the Jews cried out, "If you release this man, you are not Caesar's friend. Everyone who makes himself a king opposes Caesar." ¹³ So when Pilate heard these words, he brought Jesus out and sat down on the judgment seat at a place called The Stone Pavement, and in Aramaic Gabbatha. ¹⁴ Now it was the day of Preparation of the Passover. It was about the sixth hour. He said to the Jews, "Behold your King!" ¹⁵ They cried out, "Away with him, away with him, crucify him!" Pilate said to them, "Shall I crucify your King?" The chief priests answered, "We have no king but Caesar." ¹⁶ So he delivered him over to them to be crucified.

OBSERVE

INTERPRET

KEY WORDS	DEFINITIONS	CROSS REFERENCES

MAIN POINT(S)

APPLY

PRAY

day *two*

JOHN 19:17-27

READ

So they took Jesus, [17] and he went out, bearing his own cross, to the place called The Place of a Skull, which in Aramaic is called Golgotha. [18] There they crucified him, and with him two others, one on either side, and Jesus between them. [19] Pilate also wrote an inscription and put it on the cross. It read, "Jesus of Nazareth, the King of the Jews." [20] Many of the Jews read this inscription, for the place where Jesus was crucified was near the city, and it was written in Aramaic, in Latin, and in Greek. [21] So the chief priests of the Jews said to Pilate, "Do not write, 'The King of the Jews,' but rather, 'This man said, I am King of the Jews.'" [22] Pilate answered, "What I have written I have written."

[23] When the soldiers had crucified Jesus, they took his garments and divided them into four parts, one part for each soldier; also his tunic. But the tunic was seamless, woven in one piece from top to bottom, [24] so they said to one another, "Let us not tear it, but cast lots for it to see whose it shall be." This was to fulfill the Scripture which says,

"They divided my garments among them,
    and for my clothing they cast lots."

So the soldiers did these things, [25] but standing by the cross of Jesus were his mother and his mother's sister, Mary the wife of Clopas, and Mary Magdalene. [26] When Jesus saw his mother and the disciple whom he loved standing nearby, he said to his mother, "Woman, behold, your son!" [27] Then he said to the disciple, "Behold, your mother!" And from that hour the disciple took her to his own home.

OBSERVE

INTERPRET

KEY WORDS	DEFINITIONS	CROSS REFERENCES

MAIN POINT(S)

APPLY

PRAY

day *three*

JOHN 19:28-37

READ	OBSERVE	INTERPRET
²⁸ Ater this, Jesus, knowing that all was now finished, said (to fulfill the Scripture), "I thirst." ²⁹ A jar full of sour wine stood there, so they put a sponge full of the sour wine on a hyssop branch and held it to his mouth. ³⁰ When Jesus had received the sour wine, he said, "It is finished," and he bowed his head and gave up his spirit. ³¹ Since it was the day of Preparation, and so that the bodies would not remain on the cross on the Sabbath (for that Sabbath was a high day), the Jews asked Pilate that their legs might be broken and that they might be taken away. ³² So the soldiers came and broke the legs of the first, and of the other who had been crucified with him. ³³ But when they came to Jesus and saw that he was already dead, they did not break his legs. ³⁴ But one of the soldiers pierced his side with a spear, and at once there came out blood and water. ³⁵ He who saw it has borne witness— his testimony is true, and he knows that he is telling the truth—that you also may believe. ³⁶ For these things took place that the Scripture might be fulfilled: "Not one of his bones will be broken." ³⁷ And again another Scripture says, "They will look on him whom they have pierced."		

KEY WORDS	DEFINITIONS	CROSS REFERENCES

MAIN POINT(S)	APPLY

PRAY

day *four*

READ	OBSERVE	INTERPRET
38 After these things Joseph of Arimathea, who was a disciple of Jesus, but secretly for fear of the Jews, asked Pilate that he might take away the body of Jesus, and Pilate gave him permission. So he came and took away his body. 39 Nicodemus also, who earlier had come to Jesus by night, came bringing a mixture of myrrh and aloes, about seventy-five pounds in weight. 40 So they took the body of Jesus and bound it in linen cloths with the spices, as is the burial custom of the Jews. 41 Now in the place where he was crucified there was a garden, and in the garden a new tomb in which no one had yet been laid. 42 So because of the Jewish day of Preparation, since the tomb was close at hand, they laid Jesus there.		

KEY WORDS	DEFINITIONS	CROSS REFERENCES

MAIN POINT(S)

APPLY

PRAY

day *five*

JOHN 19 | REVIEW & DISCUSSION QUESTIONS

Summary:	Write out a favorite verse(s) from the passage, perhaps in your own words:
In what specific ways is Jesus mocked as king?	In verse 5, Pilate exclaims, "Behold the man!" In what ways does this statement summarize the chapter and in some ways the Gospel of John?
How does seeing Jesus in this way impact our own understanding of God's presence in the midst of our suffering?	Explain what Jesus says about "power?" (19:10-11)

Why are the chief priests upset about Pilate's inscription? What is the irony?

What is so appalling about the chief priests answer of, "We have no king but Caesar?"

Personally, what is the significance of Jesus's words, "It is finished?"

What do you learn about Joseph and Nicodemus from their actions?

Why is it significant the Jesus's death fulfilled so many OT prophecies? How does it help us understand God's plan and faithfulness to us?

Praise God for at least one truth from this week's study:

WHEN JESUS HAD RECEIVED
THE SOUR WINE, HE SAID,
"IT IS FINISHED," AND HE
BOWED HIS HEAD AND
GAVE UP HIS SPIRIT.

JOHN 19:30

week *twenty-two*

LESSON 21: JOHN 20

day *one*

JOHN 20:1-10

READ	OBSERVE	INTERPRET
[1] Now on the first day of the week Mary Magdalene came to the tomb early, while it was still dark, and saw that the stone had been taken away from the tomb. [2] So she ran and went to Simon Peter and the other disciple, the one whom Jesus loved, and said to them, "They have taken the Lord out of the tomb, and we do not know where they have laid him." [3] So Peter went out with the other disciple, and they were going toward the tomb. [4] Both of them were running together, but the other disciple outran Peter and reached the tomb first. [5] And stooping to look in, he saw the linen cloths lying there, but he did not go in. [6] Then Simon Peter came, following him, and went into the tomb. He saw the linen cloths lying there, [7] and the face cloth, which had been on Jesus's head, not lying with the linen cloths but folded up in a place by itself. [8] Then the other disciple, who had reached the tomb first, also went in, and he saw and believed; [9] for as yet they did not understand the Scripture, that he must rise from the dead. [10] Then the disciples went back to their homes.		

KEY WORDS	DEFINITIONS	CROSS REFERENCES

MAIN POINT(S)

APPLY

PRAY

day *two*

READ	OBSERVE	INTERPRET
¹¹ But Mary stood weeping outside the tomb, and as she wept she stooped to look into the tomb. ¹² And she saw two angels in white, sitting where the body of Jesus had lain, one at the head and one at the feet. ¹³ They said to her, "Woman, why are you weeping?" She said to them, "They have taken away my Lord, and I do not know where they have laid him." ¹⁴ Having said this, she turned around and saw Jesus standing, but she did not know that it was Jesus. ¹⁵ Jesus said to her, "Woman, why are you weeping? Whom are you seeking?" Supposing him to be the gardener, she said to him, "Sir, if you have carried him away, tell me where you have laid him, and I will take him away." ¹⁶ Jesus said to her, "Mary." She turned and said to him in Aramaic, "Rabboni!" (which means Teacher). ¹⁷ Jesus said to her, "Do not cling to me, for I have not yet ascended to the Father; but go to my brothers and say to them, 'I am ascending to my Father and your Father, to my God and your God.'" ¹⁸ Mary Magdalene went and announced to the disciples, "I have seen the Lord"—and that he had said these things to her.		

KEY WORDS	DEFINITIONS	CROSS REFERENCES

MAIN POINT(S)

APPLY

PRAY

day *three*

READ	OBSERVE	INTERPRET
[19] On the evening of that day, the first day of the week, the doors being locked where the disciples were for fear of the Jews, Jesus came and stood among them and said to them, "Peace be with you." [20] When he had said this, he showed them his hands and his side. Then the disciples were glad when they saw the Lord. [21] Jesus said to them again, "Peace be with you. As the Father has sent me, even so I am sending you." [22] And when he had said this, he breathed on them and said to them, "Receive the Holy Spirit. [23] If you forgive the sins of any, they are forgiven them; if you withhold forgiveness from any, it is withheld."		

KEY WORDS	DEFINITIONS	CROSS REFERENCES

MAIN POINT(S)

APPLY

PRAY

day *four*

READ	OBSERVE	INTERPRET
²⁴ Now Thomas, one of the twelve, called the Twin, was not with them when Jesus came. ²⁵ So the other disciples told him, "We have seen the Lord." But he said to them, "Unless I see in his hands the mark of the nails, and place my finger into the mark of the nails, and place my hand into his side, I will never believe." ²⁶ Eight days later, his disciples were inside again, and Thomas was with them. Although the doors were locked, Jesus came and stood among them and said, "Peace be with you." ²⁷ Then he said to Thomas, "Put your finger here, and see my hands; and put out your hand, and place it in my side. Do not disbelieve, but believe." ²⁸ Thomas answered him, "My Lord and my God!" ²⁹ Jesus said to him, "Have you believed because you have seen me? Blessed are those who have not seen and yet have believed." ³⁰ Now Jesus did many other signs in the presence of the disciples, which are not written in this book; ³¹ but these are written so that you may believe that Jesus is the Christ, the Son of God, and that by believing you may have life in his name.		

KEY WORDS	DEFINITIONS	CROSS REFERENCES

MAIN POINT(S)

APPLY

PRAY

day *five*

JOHN 20 | REVIEW & DISCUSSION QUESTIONS

Summary:	Write out a favorite verse(s) from the passage, perhaps in your own words:
When Mary Magdalene sees the stone rolled away from the tomb, what is her first reaction?	What evidence of Christ's resurrection does John present?
What is significant to you about how Jesus refers to God in verse 17?	In verse 21, what do you learn about the mission that Jesus gives His followers?

How did Jesus deal with Thomas's doubt?	What can we learn from Thomas's experience?
What is John's purpose in writing this book? (20:30-31)	Has your belief in Christ benefited by this study of the Gospel of John? Has your faith been strengthened? How so?
How does the historical resurrection of Jesus Christ - that He died and rose again and is alive - influence your personal attitude and choices this week?	Praise God for at least one truth from this week's study:

BLESSED ARE THOSE WHO
HAVE NOT SEEN AND YET
HAVE BELIEVED.

JOHN 20:29

week *twenty-three*

LESSON 22: JOHN 21

day *one*

JOHN 21:1-8

READ	OBSERVE	INTERPRET
¹ After this Jesus revealed himself again to the disciples by the Sea of Tiberias, and he revealed himself in this way. ² Simon Peter, Thomas (called the Twin), Nathanael of Cana in Galilee, the sons of Zebedee, and two others of his disciples were together. ³ Simon Peter said to them, "I am going fishing." They said to him, "We will go with you." They went out and got into the boat, but that night they caught nothing. ⁴ Just as day was breaking, Jesus stood on the shore; yet the disciples did not know that it was Jesus. ⁵ Jesus said to them, "Children, do you have any fish?" They answered him, "No." ⁶ He said to them, "Cast the net on the right side of the boat, and you will find some." So they cast it, and now they were not able to haul it in, because of the quantity of fish. ⁷ That disciple whom Jesus loved therefore said to Peter, "It is the Lord!" When Simon Peter heard that it was the Lord, he put on his outer garment, for he was stripped for work, and threw himself into the sea. ⁸ The other disciples came in the boat, dragging the net full of fish, for they were not far from the land, but about a hundred yards off.		

KEY WORDS	DEFINITIONS	CROSS REFERENCES

MAIN POINT(S)	APPLY

PRAY

day *two*

JOHN 21:9-14

READ	OBSERVE	INTERPRET
[9] When they got out on land, they saw a charcoal fire in place, with fish laid out on it, and bread. [10] Jesus said to them, "Bring some of the fish that you have just caught." [11] So Simon Peter went aboard and hauled the net ashore, full of large fish, 153 of them. And although there were so many, the net was not torn. [12] Jesus said to them, "Come and have breakfast." Now none of the disciples dared ask him, "Who are you?" They knew it was the Lord. [13] Jesus came and took the bread and gave it to them, and so with the fish. [14] This was now the third time that Jesus was revealed to the disciples after he was raised from the dead.		

KEY WORDS	DEFINITIONS	CROSS REFERENCES

MAIN POINT(S)

APPLY

PRAY

day *three*

JOHN 21:15-19

READ	OBSERVE	INTERPRET
¹⁵ When they had finished breakfast, Jesus said to Simon Peter, "Simon, son of John, do you love me more than these?" He said to him, "Yes, Lord; you know that I love you." He said to him, "Feed my lambs." ¹⁶ He said to him a second time, "Simon, son of John, do you love me?" He said to him, "Yes, Lord; you know that I love you." He said to him, "Tend my sheep." ¹⁷ He said to him the third time, "Simon, son of John, do you love me?" Peter was grieved because he said to him the third time, "Do you love me?" and he said to him, "Lord, you know everything; you know that I love you." Jesus said to him, "Feed my sheep. ¹⁸ Truly, truly, I say to you, when you were young, you used to dress yourself and walk wherever you wanted, but when you are old, you will stretch out your hands, and another will dress you and carry you where you do not want to go." ¹⁹ (This he said to show by what kind of death he was to glorify God.) And after saying this he said to him, "Follow me."		

KEY WORDS	DEFINITIONS	CROSS REFERENCES

MAIN POINT(S)

APPLY

PRAY

day *four*

READ	OBSERVE	INTERPRET
²⁰ Peter turned and saw the disciple whom Jesus loved following them, the one who also had leaned back against him during the supper and had said, "Lord, who is it that is going to betray you?" ²¹ When Peter saw him, he said to Jesus, "Lord, what about this man?" ²² Jesus said to him, "If it is my will that he remain until I come, what is that to you? You follow me!" ²³ So the saying spread abroad among the brothers that this disciple was not to die; yet Jesus did not say to him that he was not to die, but, "If it is my will that he remain until I come, what is that to you?" ²⁴ This is the disciple who is bearing witness about these things, and who has written these things, and we know that his testimony is true. ²⁵ Now there are also many other things that Jesus did. Were every one of them to be written, I suppose that the world itself could not contain the books that would be written.		

KEY WORDS	DEFINITIONS	CROSS REFERENCES

MAIN POINT(S)

APPLY

PRAY

day *five*

JOHN 21 | REVIEW & DISCUSSION QUESTIONS

Summary:	Write out a favorite verse(s) from the passage, perhaps in your own words:
How do the disciples recognize Jesus?	How might the fishing story relate to our work and projects?
Any idea why a charcoal fire might be significant? Where else was there this type of fire?	If you were Peter, how would you feel if the Lord continued to ask, "Do you love me?"

Why does Jesus continue to ask Peter this question? Why have this be a public conversation?	Why is love an essential ingredient for Peter's mission?
Why do you think Peter continues to respond to Jesus, "You know that...?"	Why does Jesus deny Peter the information he seeks concerning John?
From verses 24-25, what do you learn about sharing the gospel message?	Praise God for at least one truth from this week's study:

...THE WORLD ITSELF COULD
NOT CONTAIN THE BOOKS
THAT WOULD BE WRITTEN.

JOHN 21:25

week *twenty-four*

LESSON 23: REVIEW

take *note*

REVIEWING THE GOSPEL OF JOHN

NOTE: Ideally for this week's review, read straight through the Gospel of John. This will help to place all the pieces together in context. If time does not permit, try taking time to glance through your notes.

take *note*

REVIEWING THE GOSPEL OF JOHN

take *note*

REVIEWING THE GOSPEL OF JOHN

take *note*

REVIEWING THE GOSPEL OF JOHN

day *five*

THE GOSPEL OF JOHN | REVIEW & DISCUSSION QUESTIONS

How would you summarize John's Gospel?	What favorite verses will you now carry with you?
John had many themes that ran throughout his gospel account. Which one was your favorite? Explain.	Do you have a favorite name of God used by John?
What was a favorite or especially meaningful lesson to you from this study? Please explain.	Other than Christ, is there a particular person with whom you made a heart connection from John's account?

What new things have you learned about being a "follower of Christ?"	After this study, would your explanation of "Who is Jesus?" be different than before? How so?
Remember John's purpose for writing this gospel. (20:31) Did he fulfill his purpose? Why or why not?	John desired us to "believe." Has your personal belief and faith in Christ grown from this study? Please share a specific example.
Other thoughts:	After studying the gospel of John, I praise and thank God for:

THESE ARE WRITTEN
SO THAT YOU MAY
BELIEVE...

JOHN 20:31

Made in the USA
Las Vegas, NV
23 February 2022

44423423R00188